Zach is an amazing man, mentor, leader, and now author. He is filled with wisdom, knowledge, and faith far beyond his years.

Ben Roethlisberger
Two-time Super Bowl-winning and Six-time Pro Bowl Quarterback of the Pittsburgh Steelers

Even If reminds us that no matter the circumstances we find ourselves in, we have a choice—to get bitter or better. Zach's message is packed full of challenge and hope to rise up, break through, and live a life that's Built Different.

Jon Gordon
Fifteen-time Best-selling Author of *The Energy Bus* and *The One Truth*

I've watched Zach grow up. I've watched him compete. I've watched his life and his testimony. He gets it, and he keeps the main thing the main thing. The message of this book is anchored in the good news of the gospel and filled with a message of resilience to help you win at the big game of life.

Darryl Strawberry
Four-time MLB World Series Champion, Evangelist

A rising voice among and for today's generations, Zach gets it. As a counselor and coach, he understands pain and the principles for how to keep hope alive and persevere. His passion flows out of the source of his strength—a deep love for God and others. *Even if* is a gift to us all.

Rebekah Lyons
Best-selling Author of *Rhythms of Renewal* and
Building a Resilient Life

I love the incredibly powerful and inspiring message in *Even If* —that even if life gets hard, we can develop a mindset to keep showing up and standing up for what we believe in. And when we do so, we lift ourselves up and make a bigger difference in life.

Daniel Amen, MD
Best-selling Author of *Change Your Brain Every Day*

When everything was on the line, you wanted Zach on the mound, at the plate, taking the shot, or with the football in his hands. He's a gamer. That doesn't mean he always won or had success, but you knew he would give you all he had . . . to the very end. And yes, he knows adversity. Through the years, he battled each step of the way, which only made him stronger, helped build within him an "even if" mindset, and taught him that life is all about relationships with God and others—"friends in and for the fire."

Those who know Zach best would describe him as bold in his faith, respectful, gracious, and "up for the challenge." It started young when he had to face his fears and learn that success takes outworking everyone on the field or the court every day.

What a ride we've had together, and I have a feeling the best is yet to be. What I love most about my son is that he brings that same approach to everyday life, those he leads and serves, and to the pages of this book. I can't wait to see how God is going to continue to use him and this book for His glory.

Dr. Tim Clinton
President of the American Association of Christian Counselors

Zach Clinton's pursuit of what really matters is wrapped up in this book. As a player and a leader on our campus for many years, Zach has encouraged me. He has the perfect perspective of where we need to center our lives to be what God has created us to be. *Even If* is a must-read!

Scott Jackson
Liberty University Head Baseball Coach

Zach is undeniably anointed. He is a magnetic communicator in all domains and the Lord's spearhead of truth for the next generation. Incorporating his expertise in psychology and years of experience in the world of collegiate and professional athletics, Zach's new book *Even If* is a must-read for those who are ready to "find the setup in the setback."

Shelene Bryan
Author & Founder of Skip1.org

In a world where we'd rather be entertained than challenged, Zach Clinton places a demand upon us to prepare for battle . . . allowing no room for excuses! After reading this book, I've intentionally added two words to my daily vocabulary: *EVEN IF!* If faith is the hallmark of our Christian heritage, the evidence of that inheritance is a divinely indomitable spirit to persevere. Zach compels us to ignite that spirit! To imagine the possibilities! To dare to be different! The wisdom of this book *will* shift your mindset from *'only if'* to *'EVEN IF!'*

Dr. Rick Rigsby
Motivational Speaker, Minister, and Best-selling Author
of *Lessons From a Third-Grade Dropout*

EVEN IF

DEVELOPING THE **FAITH, MINDSET, STRENGTH** AND **ENDURANCE** OF THOSE WHO ARE **BUILT DIFFERENT**

ZACH CLINTON

WITH: **MAX DAVIS** FOREWORD BY: **TIM TIMBERLAKE**

ISBNs:
Book: 978-1-960624-05-5
Ebook: 978-1-960624-06-2

Cover design by Trent Haddock, Thursdays & Co.

Interior formatting by Anne McLaughlin, Blue Lake Design, www.bluelakedesign.com

Published by American Association of Christian Counselors Publishing

Printed in the United States

To my wife, Evelyn. I love you with every fiber of my being. I pray that the principles in this book will be the heartbeat of our marriage and our family for all of our days.

To my parents, Tim and Julie. No words could ever express my gratitude for you. This book would not have been possible without the love and devotion you've invested in me and the example you continually display of an "even if" faith, mindset, and endurance.

CONTENTS

FOREWORD

I n a world where convenience often trumps commitment and the allure of immediate gratification overshadows enduring faith, an inspiring call resounds through the pages of *Even If*. This book is a testament to uncommon faith, strength, and endurance, and it beckons readers to embrace a paradigm shift that transcends the ordinary.

The narrative begins with a powerful juxtaposition of the "even if" mindset against the more commonplace "only if." The distinction is stark—a choice between transactional bargains with God and an unwavering commitment to trust God in the face of adversity. The foundational passage, echoing the resolve of three men in the fiery furnace, sets the tone for a journey that transcends circumstances, going beyond the limits of human expectation.

Drawing from personal experiences and timeless truths, Zach Clinton unveils a transformative perspective on hope. Anchored in the profound belief that hope is not an abstract concept but a person, a name—Jesus. This revelation becomes the linchpin for an "even if" mindset, strength, and endurance. The narrative skillfully weaves through the tapestry of life's challenges, offering solace to the broken-hearted and directing those searching for hope.

The book offers a blueprint for navigating life's inevitable storms—acknowledging the fact that pain is unavoidable but not permanent. This wisdom goes far beyond mere optimism; it is rooted in the assurance that courage, fueled by the Spirit within, is a distinguishing mark of those who are Built Different. The metaphor of the buffalo running into the storm for a breakthrough becomes a clarion call to readers: face your challenges head-on, and you shall prevail.

These pages unveil principles, valuable lessons, and a call to action. Zach's genuine passion for the broken-hearted is palpable, and his desire to walk alongside individuals in their darkest moments permeates every word. This is not just a book; it's a journey of self-discovery, resilience, and transformation.

As you embark on the pages of *Even If*, let it be an invitation to reshape your perspective so you can embrace the mantra: *"Even if* circumstances aren't what I expected, I'll trust God." The narrative unfolds as a partnership, with Zach planting seeds of wisdom, urging readers to plow their paths, and trusting in a higher power to provide a harvest in due time.

So, which way are you running? In a world fraught with challenges and uncertainties, this book serves as a compass, guiding you to run toward your storms, equipped with unwavering faith, a resilient mindset, unmatched strength, and prevailing endurance. Let the journey begin—not in the pursuit of *what if*, but in the unyielding resolve of *even if*. Let's roll into a future defined by faith, courage, and an unshakeable commitment to be built different.

Tim Timberlake
Lead Pastor of Celebration Church and Best-selling
Author of *The Power of 1440* and *The Art of Overcoming*

ONE

THE CHOICE IS YOURS

"Even if everyone is doing it, wrong is never right."
— **Russell M. Nelson**

Growing up, I played three sports—football in the fall, basketball in the winter, and baseball all spring and summer long. Every kid who walks out on a field or a court of any kind has dreams of one day competing at the highest level and excelling at just the right moment: catching a deflected Hail Mary pass to score the winning touchdown . . . nailing a three-point buzzer beater to come from behind at the very last second . . . or hitting a walk-off home run in the championship game. I had all those dreams, but baseball was my primary love.

I started playing when I was just five years old at the Forest Recreation Center in central Virginia. I can't tell you how many summer hours I spent on a ball field or in a batting cage, grinding every day. I devoted much time, effort, and attention to become my very best, and some of my fondest childhood memories were the days spent at travel ball tournaments with my best friends— guys who remained best friends throughout my life. They were always in my corner, and I will always be in theirs.

My baseball playing career progressed from Dixie youth, to travel ball, to high school, and then, thankfully, getting the opportunity to play at the Division 1 level. It was a seemingly endless positive experience as I learned valuable lessons, won championships, received accolades, and made some wild lifetime memories. I knew that baseball is also a game of adversity where you often have to battle through challenge and difficulty, but I was yet to discover how low it could take me.

I signed as a junior in high school to play college baseball at Liberty University. The higher you go in athletic competition, the more the skill gap closes between players, the speed accelerates, and the challenge grows . . . so do expectations and the drive to excel and keep the dream alive. My freshman year I found myself pitching against programs like Kennesaw State (rated #17 that year), the University of North Carolina (#8), the University of Virginia (#5), and many more. Game on! I was soaking in every opportunity and having the time of my life.

In the spring of my sophomore year, I was practicing in the bullpen, preparing to start the new season in two weeks. I was planning to take a couple of more pitches before wrapping up for the day, and on one pitch my foot slipped a little too far past my landing spot. I felt a twinge in my knee, and a few days later the doctors told me I'd suffered an *avulsion fracture* on the head of my fibula. They said I was going to be out for the season. Just like that, everything I had worked so hard for and spent countless hours preparing for that year was stripped away in the snap of a finger. Game over. Season over.

I'll be honest with you. When I was given the news that I wasn't going to be able to compete with my best friends and teammates in that upcoming baseball season, a bomb went off inside me. I was devastated. I had never been in that position before. For several days, I was intensely frustrated and upset, not just with the situation, but with life.

I'm sure you've had experiences where your life was breezing along but then something happened that sent you crashing to the ground, emotionally, spiritually, and/or physically. Of course, I realize that many of you would be thrilled if getting benched for a season during your adolescence was the worst thing that ever happened to you. The problems we deal with as adults are much more potentially devastating: a cancer diagnosis or sudden stroke; an unfaithful spouse; loss of a job and financial security; a loved and affectionate child who falls victim to drug addiction; and the list goes on and on. How do you tend to respond in those situations?

It's quite natural for us to look for someone to blame, and when we can't point a finger at anyone else, God often gets the blame. We aren't able to handle all our accumulating frustration, pain, rage, and depression, so our complaints are directed to heaven: "Are you serious, God?! Why me?! I've worked hard! I don't deserve this! This isn't fair!" Or we start bargaining with God: "If You will just heal, or provide, or perform a miracle, then I promise to stay true to You and Your Word." But even beyond that comes the next inevitable question: what happens if what you're looking for, praying for, waiting for, and hoping for doesn't come to pass? What then? Will you still praise His name, live a life of faith, and be there to encourage those around you? Or does your life take a turn as you allow bitterness to take root, where every new disappointment only adds to your misery?

Thankfully, I had loving parents who steered me through my first big crisis. I'll never forget the moment my dad pulled me aside and said, "Bud, I know you're discouraged, and I know you're disappointed with the circumstances, but you can't control those things. However, the one thing you *can* control is how you respond. So, I want you to make a choice—you can hang out and let this season slip through your fingers, or you can work out and make the most of this season by allowing God to do His work in and through you as He shapes, molds, and develops you into the man and leader He wants you to become."

My dad has always been my hero. At the age of twenty-eight, I still jokingly say that I want to grow up to be just like him, but the truth is, I mean that with my whole heart. I'm following in his footsteps. He's the President of the American Association of Christian Counselors (AACC), and I've worked hard to become a Vice President in that organization that I have so much respect for. I'm also trying to emulate my dad in other ways. He's a man of consistency, humility, moral character, and drive. He is unwaveringly devoted to his faith, family, and those he loves. He lives out what he preaches every single day. He learned those traits from a great dad of his own, whom we all call Papa C—one of the kindest and most caring men I've ever known. A man of great integrity and loyalty, Papa C fiercely loved God, his family, and all those he had the opportunity of interacting with. These men, my heroes, bring me inspiration every day. I often ponder the sage advice I've received from them throughout the years of my life. Even when I was young, my dad challenged me to start working out not just to improve my physical strength, but also my mindset, my relationships, and my walk and faith in Christ.

The heartbeat of this book stems from the invaluable principles and lessons I've learned from some of the hardest and most challenging moments of my life, as well as those who have impacted and influenced me—ordinary people who made an extraordinary decision to stay true to their faith rather than succumbing to the expectations, opinions, or circumstances around them. I now regularly share these principles with athletes, leaders, and clients.

A TRULY FIERY TRIAL

While growing up, one of my favorite Bible stories was the account of Shadrach, Meshach, and Abednego. They were Jewish exiles taken into captivity in Babylon to serve Nebuchadnezzar, the king over the empire. When they arrived, their devotion to God made them stand out from all Nebuchadnezzar's other servants and counselors (Daniel 1:20). But then one day Nebuchadnezzar erected an image of gold that was approximately ninety feet tall by nine feet wide (perhaps of himself), and he assembled a large assortment of musicians and instruments. He summoned all the officials of the land for the dedication of the golden statue, and ordered them to fall and worship the image when they heard the music play. The time came, the music sounded, and all the officials bowed . . . all but three men.

Some of King Nebuchadnezzar's brown-nosing fan club quickly brought to his attention the three men who had paid no attention to his orders. Furious with rage and probably a hint of embarrassment and humiliation, Nebuchadnezzar summoned those audacious men into his presence with threats and one more opportunity to save themselves:

"Is it true, Shadrach, Meshach, and Abednego, that you do not serve my gods or worship the image of gold I have set up? Now when you hear the sound of the horn, flute, zither, lyre, harp, pipe and all kinds of music, if you are ready to fall down and worship the image I made, very good. But if you do not worship it, you will be thrown immediately into a blazing furnace. Then what god will be able to rescue you from my hand?" (Daniel 3:14-15)

At that point, most people would have weighed their impassioned moral stand against the almost certain death sentence, concluding that it would be okay to bow just this once and ask God's forgiveness later. Yet with full acknowledgment of the penalty awaiting them, these three men stood their ground and said:

> "King Nebuchadnezzar, we do not need to defend ourselves before you in this matter. If we are thrown into the blazing furnace, the God we serve is able to deliver us from it, and he will deliver us from Your Majesty's hand. But *even if* he does not, we want you to know, Your Majesty, that we will not serve your gods or worship the image of gold you have set up." (Daniel 3:16-18, emphasis added)

"ONLY IF . . ." VS. "EVEN IF . . ."

The difference between "even if" and "only if" is enormous. One perspective keeps us distanced from God; the other requires tremendous faith, but brings us closer to Him. Far more people are "only if" individuals. They are quick to trade away what they need most for what they want now. When tough times come, they bargain with God, promising to remain true to Him . . . only if they get what they are asking for . . . only if things turn out in their favor . . . only if the demands on them are minimal.

In contrast, the few who develop an "even if" relationship with God possess an uncommon mindset of faith, courage, and endurance. They stay true to their values, commitments, and promises regardless of how their circumstances change. They keep showing up and standing up . . . even if things don't go their way . . . even if their back is pressed up against a wall . . . even if they get criticized . . . even if they get no recognition or affirmation . . . even if their stand for God results in rejection by others.

When I think of "even if" people, one of the first names that comes to mind is Rick Rigsby, a dear friend of mine whose wife Trina was called home to be with the Lord after a long bout with breast cancer. Rick had to watch her suffer and battle every single day for months, and then eventually had to grieve her death. After such a lengthy period of praying for his wife's recovery, he found himself at the foot of her casket weeping and crying out to God. His dad walked over and wrapped his arms around his son, to console him. Rick looked up at his father and said, "Dad, I feel like I've lost hope." His father responded, "Son, you can't lose something that God gave you. You haven't lost hope. You've just lost perspective." Rick has shared this story with people around the globe, and God's message through his dad continues to bless others.

A SURPRISE ENDING

I would venture to say that several of you reading this book right now have somehow lost perspective on your life and feel as if you are desperately searching for hope. Whether it be due to a season- or career-ending injury, the loss of a loved one, or something else, maybe you just don't know where to turn. Before going any farther, let me share with you the most important thing you need to know: hope is a person, and hope has a name. His name is Jesus. I don't think you can ever develop an *even if* mindset apart from that fact, because it is the truth that has shifted my perspective, ignited my patience and purpose, provided much-needed strength and endurance, and sustained the perseverance to keep going.

This book has really opened my eyes to the work God has done in and through me thanks to the growth I've experienced during some of the hardest moments of my life. Beyond anything else, I want you to know this: if you're battling a hardship right now and feel pressed on all sides to the point of being crushed, you are not alone. You should always have hope because God is always with you!

But don't take my word for it. When Shadrach, Meshach, and Abednego refused to bow down to the king's image, Nebuchadnezzar became furious. He had the furnace heated to seven times its usual intensity, and ordered them to be bound and thrown in. The blast killed the soldiers who followed his orders, but Shadrach, Meshach, and Abednego were soon seen walking around in the flames . . . along with a fourth figure described as looking like "a son of the gods." The king called for them to come out. They were unbound and unharmed, without as much as a singed hair (Daniel 3:19-27).

Indeed, the Son of God walks with us through the fiery trials of our lives. We serve a God of grace and forgiveness, who never gives up on us. He gave His one and only Son to come to this world not to be served, but to serve and to give His life as a ransom for many (Matthew 20:28). Jesus lived a sinless and blameless life, died a substitutionary death on a cross in our place, and rose again three days later. In doing so, He defeated sin and death, providing us the opportunity of believing and accepting Him as the personal Lord and Savior of our lives. How great is the Father's love for us. No one is worthy of all He has done for us, yet we hold the position of "children of God" (1 John 3:1).

God doesn't ask or expect us to be perfect. He died for us while we were still sinners (Romans 5:8). Your life may be in shambles and you see no way out of the mess you're in, but He just asks you to be open and willing to receive the unspeakable and free gift He has for you. As you go through this book, I encourage you to invite God to come closer and reveal what He has prepared for you.

I have a real heart and passion for those motivated to perform at their best, those battling for a breakthrough, and those who are living in a dark or difficult season in life. I want to walk alongside and strengthen those who are in their deepest and darkest seasons of pain and remind them that they are never alone. I believe God not only equips us with friends for the fire, but He will always be the "fourth man" in the flames as well. So even if you're discouraged, even if you've made some mistakes, even if you haven't seen any progress toward resolving your painful trial, I pray that the lessons and principles within the upcoming pages can help you do exactly that. These are some of the focal points and principles I've shared with countless people in high schools, colleges, churches, companies and organizations, and collegiate and professional locker rooms. My desire is to help you reshape your perspective and discover what it truly means to live by the mantra "even if . . ." Stop worrying about "what if . . .?" Stop trying to negotiate with God for "only if . . ." Determine here and now to muster the faith and courage to pursue an ongoing mindset of "even if . . ." We'll work together to do the planting. Individually, you'll do the plowing. And we'll trust God to provide the harvest in His will and in His timing! Let's roll!

TWO

WHICH WAY ARE YOU RUNNING?

"When I thought I was going to die,
I fought differently."

— Marcus Luttrell

Mortars exploding. Shards of rock flying. Smoke. Fire. Trees down. Shrapnel. A steady stream of rapid gunfire pelting down like heavy rain. Taliban fighters were hidden everywhere—behind trees and boulders, and in caves high up in the jagged 10,000-foot Hindu Kush mountains outside Asadabad, Afghanistan. On the mountainside below, taking cover in a rocky ravine, was a four-man Navy SEAL team consisting of the officer-in-charge, Lieutenant Michael Murphy, along with Hospital Corpsman 2nd Class Marcus Luttrell, Gunner's Mate 2nd Class Danny Dietz, and Sonar Technician 2nd Class Matthew Axelson.

The Taliban outnumbered the SEAL team some fifty to four, and because they were higher up the ridge, they were in a better position to hit their targets. Eventually, the bullets raining down began to take their toll. All four SEALS were wounded and tried to retreat by sliding and jumping down the steep rocky ledges, causing additional injuries including deep gashes and broken bones. Leaning against a boulder with bullets ricocheting around them, Murphy and Luttrell were both losing blood from multiple wounds. Murphy turned to his buddy with a penetrating look and said, "Marcus . . . you're *never* out of the fight."[1] Luttrell responded with terror-filled eyes and a slight nod of affirmation. Giving up was never a consideration.

Meanwhile, Dietz was scouring the area for a clearing in the trees where he could make a distress call back to the base. But before he could secure a place, he was shot in the hand, shattering it and rendering him unable to complete the task. Murphy saw what happened and knew what he had to do. He could see another open spot on a cliff edge where he could make the call . . . if he could get there. It would enable the military operations to locate their position on the grid and send in forces to save his brothers, but it would also place him directly in the enemy's line of fire, almost certain to cost him his life.

Murphy took a deep breath and then bolted to the cliff's open edge. With everything on the line, under a barrage of gunfire, he contacted the SOF Quick Reaction Force at Bagram Air Base, requested assistance, and gave his unit's location. Even as he was making the call, enemy bullets burned into his back, further wounding him. Amazingly, he had the composure to complete the transmission before staggering back to his position of cover and continue returning fire.

Murphy's transmission was received and a helicopter with eight more SEALs and eight Army Night Stalkers was quickly dispatched. However, as the helicopter wove its way through the mountain terrain toward the four surrounded SEALs, a rocket-propelled grenade struck it, killing everyone aboard.

Murphy, Luttrell, Dietz, and Axelson continued fighting for their lives. Two hours later, some thirty-five Taliban were dead, but so were Murphy, Axelson, and Dietz. Only Marcus Luttrell had survived, though he was severely wounded and temporarily unconscious due to a nearby blast. After regaining consciousness, he was able to escape by inching slowly down the side of a cliff. For the next day, Luttrell continued to evade the remaining Taliban. With shrapnel embedded in both legs, a bullet wound in one, and several broken vertebrae in his back, he trekked on foot for seven miles. I can't help but think that as Marcus Luttrell hobbled forward, he was replaying those words from Lieutenant Murphy, who had sacrificed his life for him: "Marcus . . . you're *never* out of the fight." Murphy's statement was like fuel propelling him to keep moving forward, one step after another.

As Marcus plodded along, some friendly local natives happened upon him and carried him to a nearby settlement. For three days they fed him, nursed his wounds, and protected him. When the Taliban came searching and ordered them to turn Luttrell over, they refused, even at the risk of their own lives. Luttrell scribbled a note explaining his plight and one of the natives slipped the paper into his pocket and took it to a Marine outpost. On July 2, 2005, Marcus Luttrell was rescued from enemy territory. Of his team of four, he was the lone survivor.

Obviously, Luttrell performed some heroics of his own to survive, including putting his body in the line of fire for his comrades. Yet if not for the courageous acts of Murphy, Dietz, and Axelson, the sixteen soldiers on the helicopter, and the natives who put their lives in danger, he would have never made it.[2]

What motivates me most about this story is the willingness of every individual involved to risk everything for someone else. Such action requires drive, determination, strength, valor, and sacrifice. What drives a person at this level? What separates them from others? What is wired into their hearts and minds?

What about you? Most of us aren't likely to find ourselves being shot at in the hills of Afghanistan, but think about a difficult battle you've recently faced, or are facing now. What qualities arise from deep inside you? Courage or cowardice? Action or paralysis? Faith or fear? What are you willing to do and what are you willing to give up to make a difference . . . to *be* the difference? You need to know the answers to these questions because one thing is for certain, you *will* face struggles in life.

Damon West is a former college quarterback whose meth addition led to his becoming a prison inmate known as the "Uptown Burglar." But after his life was transformed by Jesus, he became one of the world's most popular authors and motivational speakers. Among his sage advice, he writes, "You don't have to win all your fights, but you must fight all your fights."[3]

STORM WARNING

It may be difficult for some people to think of the struggles in their lives as *battles*. A battle is a conflict to be won or lost, where the difference is determined by how hard we fight. Not all difficult circumstances fit that perspective. Many are what I would describe as *storms*.

You can design strategies to win battles, but when a tornado blows through your community, you can fight it as long and hard as you want, and it won't make a bit of difference. You can win battles, but all you can do with a storm is weather it.

A young child who has just been diagnosed with leukemia is in for a storm. Treatment is likely to involve years of regular shots and infusions, periods of extreme weakness and vulnerability, and isolation from friends due to low or nonexistent immunity. People talk about fighting cancer, and in a sense, it *is* a battle for the child. But for the parents, it's more of a storm. They quickly realize there's nothing to fight except their own emotions of fear and anxiety. They are helpless to do anything except wait and pray as they ride out the storm.

And it's not like we can live our lives in such a way as to avoid storms. It's been said there are basically three kinds of people in the world: those who are in the middle of a storm, those who just came out of a storm, and those who are approaching a storm. If you've just come out of a storm, take a few deep breaths, exhale, and regroup. Then, brace yourself because it won't be long before another one rolls through!

Since we can't avoid the many storms of life, we need a different strategy to cope with them, and for that I recommend we look to the buffalo for an example. It works for me. Once when I was experiencing an incredibly difficult situation, I stumbled across an eye-opening article that explained how raging storms sometimes swirl through the mountains of the Colorado Rockies—storms so thick and so dark that every animal runs away . . . except for one, the buffalo. The buffalo actually runs *into* the storm! But when you think about it, it only makes sense. Even though other animals (cattle, for instance) run away from storms, the storm inevitably catches up with them. When it does, they find themselves running in tandem with the bad weather, which prolongs their exposure to the unpleasant elements. Because the buffalo runs *into* the storm, however, it also runs *through* the storm, which allows it to get back to fair weather sooner.[4]

How about you? When the storms of your life roll in, do you try to outrun them and find yourself engulfed in the pain and suffering longer than desired, or do you take that storm head-on? Do you pray to "catch a break," or do you ask the Lord to strengthen and equip you to "take courage" for a breakthrough? In one of Eric

Thomas's critically acclaimed books, he quotes Lance Armstrong: "Pain is temporary. It may last a minute, or an hour, or a day, or a year, but eventually it will subside and something else will take its place. If I quit, however, it lasts forever."[5]

Attempting to escape the pains of life is futile. No matter how long and hard we run from them, eventually the storm will catch up, and you will only have extended your struggle. Don't try to *outrun* your pain, run *through* your pain!

Our storms vary in size and intensity, but they're a fact of life for everyone. It's not a matter of *if*, but *when*. If it sounds as if I'm being pessimistic, I would argue that I'm only being realistic. Jesus himself warned His first-century followers: "In this world you will have trouble." But He didn't stop there. Immediately, He continued: "But take heart! I have overcome the world" (John 16:33). He was trying to prepare His original disciples for very threatening storms to come. They were all about to undergo dark and difficult persecution, including flogging (Acts 5:40), imprisonment (Acts 12:2-4), and for most of them, dying a martyr's death.

And I believe Jesus was speaking to his twenty-first-century followers as well. In this world, *we* will have trouble. The Apostle James wrote, "You do not even know what will happen tomorrow. What is your life? You are a mist that appears for a little while and then vanishes" (James 4:14). Jesus and James had a different perspective on life. They didn't make decisions to see how much struggling they could avoid, and possibly live longer as a result. They realized that no matter what we do to extend our lives, we'll be gone all too soon. The point, then, is to make the most of the time we've been given.

When I realize that my life is a mere vapor, it makes me want to live as if every breath I take may be my last—that I only have a set amount of time to do what God created me to do. Life is too short to spend running from every storm and avoiding every opportunity that has the slightest risk involved. That strategy only leaves us perpetually frightened, frustrated, and confused. Whether you're fighting a boots-on-the-ground battle or running full speed into an approaching storm, you are experiencing a life that makes a difference.

It's the philosophy expressed in Tim McGraw's well-known song, "Live Like You Were Dying." I was privileged to meet Marcus Luttrell personally when he spoke at our Ignite Men's Impact Weekend a few years back. He told us that when he believed he was going to die, he fought *differently*. Luttrell was in a situation where death appeared to be inevitable and immediate, but that need not be the case for everyone. Let's look at one more perspective.

DIE FIRST, AND THEN YOU CAN START TO LIVE

The Apostle Paul lived an exceptional life of self-sacrifice and commitment to Christ. He fought many battles and weathered many storms (2 Corinthians 11:21-28). Other than Jesus, perhaps no biblical character ever lived as differently as Paul did. How did he do it? Did he live like he was dying? No. He lived like he was already dead! He wrote, "I have been crucified with Christ and I no longer live, but Christ lives in me. The life I now live in the body, I live by faith in the Son of God, who loved me and gave himself for me" (Galatians 2:20).

Paul modeled what Jesus had taught His disciples: Yes, we will certainly have troubles in life, but when they come we should be courageous because He has overcome the world. We should remember that during battles *and* storms.

Sadly, some people find themselves in storms that will almost certainly last a lifetime. Perhaps you know an old couple who have been married for many decades, but where one of them has succumbed to the devastating throes of dementia. The love the other spouse feels for the afflicted one is as strong as ever as he or she takes on caregiving duties that quickly become exhausting and endless. In certain situations, no amount of tenacity, courage, or prayer is likely to defeat the disease. The healthy spouse must simply ride out the storm and ask God's will be done. Such storms require just as much courage, tenacity, and prayer as any battle—perhaps even more when you realize that the result of *this* storm/battle is predetermined. But because Jesus has overcome the world, death will never be the end for any believer. Someday every battle will be won and every storm will be over . . . for eternity.

If we can take to heart Jesus' warning that we should expect trouble, His admonition to take heart and have courage, and His assurance that He has overcome the world, we discover we begin to live *differently* and fight *differently*. All God's fullness dwells in Christ, and Christ dwells in our hearts through faith (Colossians 1:19; Ephesians 3:17). His presence is a source of courage, which is one of the foundational marks of those who are built different.

Learning to live this way influences how we view those around us, how we view ourselves, and how we view our relationships with God. It impacts how we love God and other people, as well as how we approach life. We realize that some things and some people in our lives are worth fighting and dying for. But it's not just dying for someone or something that matters most; it often takes as much courage (or more) to *live* for someone. Jesus showed His love for us when He gave the ultimate sacrifice of His life, yet if He hadn't lived a perfect life committed to God, His sacrifice would not have saved us. It takes courage to live the life God has for us and courage to live a life of love for those around us.

As we go through life, God sometimes gives us battles to fight. Like Marcus Luttrell, we might find ourselves trapped and under siege from a ruthless enemy. Those are times we need to fight . . . to resist (1 Peter 5:8-9), and He always provides the armor we need to persevere and overcome (Ephesians 6:10-18). Other times, storms will come and you will feel helpless to do anything except wait for Jesus to provide much-desired peace (Mark 4:39). Many in our culture want everyone to believe that God is either distant or weak, but the truth is that the almighty Lord of the universe has already overcome anything you're facing. He is not distant; His Spirit dwells within each believer (1 Corinthians 3:16). He is not weak; His power created the universe (Colossians 1:15-17). With Him at your side, you are *never* out of the fight.

God's love for you is fierce. He invites us to respond to His love, run into the storms of adversity, and break through to discover the life He has designed for you. Yes, it will take much courage, work, and effort, but it is through such difficulties that God forges your character, resilience, perseverance, and leadership. Your tests eventually become your testimony.

The choice is yours. You can attempt to run from the storms of life (to no avail), or you can run into those storms and come out the other side sooner . . . and stronger. Which way are you running?

THREE

A DIVIDED HEART?

"Everybody has a plan until they get
punched in the mouth."

— Mike Tyson

Mike Tyson's statement above reminds me of something C.S. Lewis wrote: "Pain insists upon being attended to. God whispers to us in our pleasures, speaks in our conscience, but shouts in our pains: it is His megaphone to rouse a deaf world."[6]

I think most of us know this from personal experience. When life is going smoothly, we can be slow to acknowledge that God is solely responsible for our daily blessings. But let things go south for a spell to the point where we're feeling the pain of loss, and suddenly God has our full attention. *What's going on, God? Why are You allowing me to suffer like this!?*

The pains of life are many and varied: debilitating diseases or other health challenges, a crumbling marriage, loss of a job, a prodigal son or daughter, death of a loved one, financial woes, a deferred dream, and more. Very often, these pains come suddenly and unexpectedly—not unlike a punch in the mouth. They are also universal; no one escapes getting knocked to the canvas from time to time. What matters, then, is how we respond *after* getting gut-punched. It may not be your fault that you get knocked to the ground in Round 1, but it *is* your fault if you're still lying there in Round 12, fretting over what happened in the first round. It's what we do with our painful moments that ultimately matters most. Our response is critical.

Pain always brings us to a fork in the road—a place where we either press into, learn, and grow from the experience, or instead begin searching for sources of relief, settling for something to anesthetize the hurt we're feeling. These unforeseen dark and difficult seasons can soon lead us to a point of desperation where we frantically seek help, hope, and encouragement. If we don't know where to turn, we become willing to try *anything* to relieve the pain, but some of our options are more harmful than helpful. That doesn't mean we're necessarily bad people, because everyone drifts off course at times. But what it does mean is that in our moments of weakness and desperation, we must be cognizant of the lies and lures our spiritual enemy will utilize. We must learn to rise above our pain by using it as a motivation to get up and keep going.

DEADLY DISTRACTIONS

Homer's *Odyssey* is the epic tale of Odysseus's return to his home in Ithaca after fighting in the Trojan War. What should have been a journey of a few weeks lasted ten years due to a series of setbacks and challenges he had to overcome. One such pit stop occurred after his boats stopped at a small island. With everyone weary and in need of refreshment, Odysseus sent three of his men to investigate the natives and look for food. The inhabitants were friendly and offered the men some of the local cuisine—flowers from the lotus plant. The flower-food was honey-sweet, and everyone who tasted it immediately lost their desire for home . . . and for anything else, wanting only to stay in the Lotus Land, eating the delectable flowers. When his men didn't return to the ships, Odysseus went to find them and had to physically drag them onboard and chain them to the ship's benches as they wept because they were being forced to leave.[7]

During one of his many times of distress, David asked God to "give me an undivided heart, that I may fear your name" (Psalm 86:11). That should be our cry, too. David understood that it is impossible to walk in God's favor if we're attempting to serve Him with a divided heart. In the Bible, the "heart" includes the complete psychological makeup of a person—mind, soul, and spirit. It's the animating center of all we do. Therefore, to have an undivided heart means your entire essence is focused and locked in on singleness of purpose.

James wrote that a "double-minded" person is "unstable" in all his or her ways (James 1:8). When something is unstable, it's wobbly, shaky, not secure. Instead of "double-minded," James could have just as well used the term "double-hearted" or "divided-heart."

David realized that a divided heart would weaken him and keep him from a proper fear of the Lord. That is, it would divide his attention between God and other desires when he really wanted to devote his whole heart to God. He realized an undivided heart translated into undivided action.

What does it mean, practically, to have an undivided heart? In David's case, just imagine how his encounter with Goliath might have turned out differently if David had timidly inched his way up to Goliath all wobbly and shaky and double-minded. I'll tell you exactly what would have happened. That first smooth stone he plucked from the brook would have surely missed its target. If it were only off a half inch or so, David would have been dead meat. Instead, the Bible says David *ran* toward Goliath (1 Samuel 17:48).

He was locked in, focused, and unafraid of the giant and the whole Philistine army! As a result, that piece of river rock nailed the target dead center, right between the eyes! David displayed no divided heart or double-mindedness, only singleness of focus and purpose.

One of the major ways the enemy divides our hearts is through *distractions*. In fact, distractions are probably the enemy's number one weapon to weaken undivided hearts. They come in many different forms. Some of the most common are distractions that arise from the cares of the world that are constantly trying to pull us away from more important things of life. Charles E. Hummel wrote in his classic pamphlet, *The Tyranny of the Urgent*, that "Your greatest danger is letting the urgent things crowd out the important."[8]

Busyness is the curse of our age. We live in an ADD society . . . perhaps literally. One expert has said our society has so many distractions that it causes people to mimic ADD symptoms. Constantly bouncing from one "urgent" matter to the next is a recipe for the ultimate overwhelmed and stressed-out life. We don't know how to be still, focus, and simply wait on the Lord.

Your most important thing in life is your foundation in Jesus. Upon that foundation is built everything else in your life: your intimacy with God, your family relationships, your purpose, and so much more. If that foundation crumbles, so does everything else that's important in life. We dare not allow urgent things (the business and busyness of life) to undermine such important matters.

Jesus warned about distractions and their potential impact: "The worries of this life, the deceitfulness of wealth and the desires for other things come in and choke the word, making it unfruitful" (Mark 4:19). The "word" spoken of here are the truths of God that produce growth and fruitfulness in our lives. How many of us can say we're never distracted by the concerns in this world, an attraction to wealth, and a craving for more and nicer things? Of course, these things are enticing, but we need not allow them to divide our hearts.

THE DEADLY ALLURE OF PLEASURE

The cares and busyness of the world can choke out God's best for our lives, to be sure, but many of those issues are essentially time problems. We know what God wants of us, but we have so many other obligations that we seldom, if ever, get around to giving Him the time we know He deserves.

Other distractions can be even more subtle and insidious: distractions that divide the heart. These types of distractions include alcohol, drugs, sex, and other temporary solutions for an innate longing or desire. They provide comfort (at first), so we don't realize how far we're drifting away from God's best for us. When our distractions become our satisfaction, they can start to destroy the trajectory of God's calling in our life. And eventually, instant gratification will always leave us unsatisfied and longing for more.

We've learned to be wary of blatant sins and addictions that we know will keep us bound and prevent us from experiencing God's fruitfulness in our lives. But I'm talking about milder distractions that are counterfeits and distortions of God's best that seem acceptable, but still keep us separated from Him. God's desire is to provide long-term fulfillment because it's what He created us to have.

C.S. Lewis said it well:

It would seem that Our Lord finds our desires not too strong, but too weak. We are half-hearted creatures, fooling about with drink and sex and ambition when infinite joy is offered us, like an ignorant child who wants to go on making mud pies

in a slum because he cannot imagine what is meant by the offer of a holiday at the sea. We are far too easily pleased.[9]

We are so often sidetracked from the infinite joy, from the amazing promises of God, that we forget about God's processes too. Sometimes God wants us to embrace and experience the processes of life to prepare us for the rewards at the end. Our goal in life should be to finish strong, not to be a shooting star that flames out. Sometimes we must take the long scenic route to get to where He wants us to be. Many times, God's best isn't clear at first, and is discovered only through faith and trust. But in the meantime, we need to stop settling for less than His best.

In the end, what is best for us is following God's will, so we should be more attentive to prevent our own wills from becoming distractions. I was recently talking with one of my mentors about why some people seem to get stuck in life and never change. What keeps them from living the life that they know they *should* be living, the life that God wants them to live? My mentor referred to John 10:10: "The thief comes only to steal and kill and destroy; I have come that they may have life, and have it to the full." Then he told me, "One of Satan's greatest accomplishments is that he tells lies that closely approximate or resemble the truth." The enemy pulls us away into distraction, divides our hearts, and ultimately causes us to miss the mark God has for our lives.

It doesn't take much to make someone miss the mark. Did you know that if a field goal kicker misses the football by less than a quarter of an inch, he can miss the field goal entirely? Therefore, the goal is making a direct foot strike every single time.

So, what makes us think that Satan wouldn't be thrilled to throw us off by just a quarter of an inch from the trajectory that God has called us to? Even the slightest distraction—the external noise of our culture and society, our circumstances, even putting our own will over the Lord's will for our life—can throw us off track by a quarter of an inch. In the long run, that tiny nudge can take us in a completely different direction from where God wanted to take us in the first place.

Satan will do anything to distract your attention, to distract your focus, to distract your eyes. We are so attention-driven that if anything comes across our horizon that looks shiny, intriguing, or pleasing, we instinctively reach for it and cling to it.

Distractions can lead to sin. Every time we sin, it pulls us away from God's best for our lives and breaks God's heart. When we better understand what sin does, I believe it will then help deter us from sinning in the first place. We overcome sin and distractions not by focusing on them and gritting our teeth while trying to overcome them on our own, but by truly releasing them to the Lord in surrender and looking to something better, to Jesus and His truth.

Dane C. Ortlund captures this point succinctly:

> We don't kill sin the way a soldier kills an enemy in battle, by zeroing in on the enemy himself. Killing sin is a strange battle because it happens by looking away from the sin. By "looking away" I don't mean emptying our minds and trying to create a mental vacuum. I mean looking at Jesus Christ. In the same way that playing matchbox cars on the front lawn loses its attractiveness when we're invited to spend the afternoon at a NASCAR race, sin loses its appeal as we allow ourselves to be re-enchanted time and again with the unsurpassable beauty of Jesus. . . . Sin feels like riches, but it is counterfeit riches, and one very quickly hits bottom on its pleasures. It doesn't deliver. Christ, on the other hand, is real riches, and one never hits bottom on them. They are unsearchable.[10]

Distractions take our focus off Jesus and onto sin. They pull us away from what's most important, God's best, and make us settle for much less. I truly believe that if we want to be built different and have a dynamic faith, it's impossible to do so without the act of surrender and authenticity. A real, enriching, deep faith in our Lord Jesus Christ comes when you recognize your brokenness and become aware of your distractions and your weaknesses. It develops when you genuinely believe that even though you've fallen off track . . . even though you may seem too far gone . . . even though God knows your every sin . . . He still loves you and calls you by name (Isaiah 43:1).

If you want to see real change in your lives, leave behind the secrets, lies, and distractions. No more white-knuckling life. No more tight fists. It's time to release it all and surrender it at the foot of the cross. It's time to let go and let God do what He's always intended to do in and through your life. It's time to be real and authentic. It's time to become the you that you've never seen before.

Lord, as David prayed, give us all an undivided heart, that we may fear Your name.

FOUR

DEADLY DABBLING

"We are too Christian really to enjoy sinning and too fond of sinning really to enjoy Christianity. Most of us know perfectly well what we ought to do; our trouble is that we do not want to do it."

— Peter Marshall

I t started with a boy and a match. Just having a little fun. Never expecting anyone to get hurt. It resulted with firefighters in full gear, risking their all . . . helicopters dumping tons of water, creating mushrooms of smoke over the blazing inferno . . . acres of forests, fields of crops, and homes and businesses all charred to the ground like burnt toast. It was one of the largest wildfires in Los Angeles County history.

On October 21, 2007, a ten-year-old boy was playing with matches and started a wildfire that spread rapidly through the dry heat, driving 15,000 people from their homes, and blackening more than 38,000 acres. It became one of the largest of fifteen simultaneous wildfires between Los Angeles and the Mexican border that resulted in seven deaths. Steve Whitmore, the detective on the case, said, "The boy acknowledged that he was playing with matches and accidentally, his words, set the fire."[11]

Really? He "accidentally" set the fire? Maybe what the boy should have said was: "I was purposely dabbling around with fire, playing with it. I only intended to strike a match or two, maybe watch a leaf or piece of paper burn, and it got out of control and turned into this gigantic wildfire. I didn't mean to do it. I tried to stop it, but couldn't. It got too big for me to handle."

But then, why should a ten-year-old boy take more responsibility than most adults who blame their bad decisions on accidents? No one wants bad things to happen. No one expects to get a divorce or commit an affair that hurts their spouse. No one intends to become an alcoholic or addict. No believer starts out thinking his or her heart will ever harden one day because of sin. But when we dabble with sin, it's like dabbling with fire. One seemingly insignificant poor choice leads to another, and then another, and before we know it, our sin nature is out of control. We feel powerless to stop it, and doomed for a life of repeated failure. We didn't intend for anything bad to happen, but we can't say it was accidental. It was a logical conclusion to a series of poor choices.

STAYING WITHIN BOUNDARIES

We must understand that sin is a perversion of God's good and proper order. The world is broken and warped because of sin and our fallen nature. When we dabble in things outside the proper, God-ordained boundaries, bad things happen. Making a fire in a fireplace creates a pleasing atmosphere, spurs creativity, brings warmth, and can cook food. But if you play around with fire, dabble with it outside the proper boundaries, it can ignite in a potentially deadly way. If not dealt with immediately, it can destroy everything in its path.

God knew this. That's why He gave us boundaries for our fallen sin nature. C. S. Lewis observes:

> Surrender to all our desires obviously leads to impotence, disease, jealousies, lies, concealment, and everything that is the reverse of health, good humour and frankness. For any happiness, even in this world, quite a lot of restraint is going to be necessary; so the claim made by every desire, when it is strong, to be healthy and reasonable, counts for nothing.[12]

Dr. Mark Laaser and my dad wrote a book titled, *The Fight of Your Life: Manning Up to the Challenge of Sexual Integrity.* Mark has since passed away, but he was one of the top sexual addiction counselors in the world. He had a private treatment/healing center in Minnesota. High profile men, particularly those in ministry, who had experienced moral failure and were locked in the vise of sexual addiction would come for extended periods to receive professional biblical counseling and healing. Many of the men had lost their families, their ministries, and reputations all because they dabbled with fire, and it got out of control. The monster grew, devoured them, and burned up what they loved most. It was common to see men falling on the floor of the clinic weeping and wailing because of the price they had paid for their foolish playing.

The problem is, when dabbling, most never think it will turn into something that gets out of control. They can handle it, they think, ignoring the challenge of Proverbs 6:27: "Can a man scoop fire into his lap without his clothes being burned?" Everyone thinks he's an exception . . . until he isn't.

The Apostle James gave a stern warning about such thinking. "Each person is tempted when they are dragged away by their own evil desire and enticed. Then, after desire has conceived, it gives birth to sin; and sin, when it is full-grown, gives birth to death" (James 1:14-15). The "death" being referred to here can take on various forms. Satan loves to make us grow numb to the convictions of the Spirit within our hearts because those convictions hold us accountable for living lives of true obedience, authenticity, and faith. When we grow numb to them, our flesh will win every time.

Do you see the progression? The sin that destroys you rarely starts big. It is conceived small, but every time it is fed, it grows stronger and larger.

"I've already done it so many times, what's once more going to hurt?"

"A little porn is not hurting anyone."

"I'll just cheat this one time."

But every time we say yes to something negative, we give it power, and the harder it becomes to say no. We get more discouraged each day, dabbling in things we shouldn't because it gets harder to stop. Then, when we least expect it, the jaws of death clamp down.

I don't know where it originated, but a wise warning that has been making the rounds for over twenty years now is that "sin fascinates and then assassinates."[13] Eve found that out the hard way, as have millions of people after her. Hopefully, we can learn from their lessons and avoid a similar consequence.

Michael O'Brien is a powerful man of God and an amazing worship leader. The former lead singer for New Song, he has several albums to his credit and performs all over the world. He has led worship for AACC's "Ignite Men's Impact Weekends," "Extraordinary Women's Events," and "World Conferences" for years. Michael has a beautiful wife and family. Porn almost ruined his life. It's no secret, and has become part of his ministry of healing to others. I interviewed him on our *Built Different* podcast. Exposed to porn when he was just seven years old, he was into hardcore stuff and a full-blown addict by age eleven. His dad wasn't present in his life to show him the way, and it all began with just one peek, just one spark that became an all-consuming wildfire. Today, it's amazing to see what a transformation is possible when someone submits to God with an undivided heart.

Maybe you've asked the question the Apostle Paul poses as a potential loophole for your errant, sinful behavior: "Since God is a God of grace, can't I just continue to live a lifestyle of sin knowing He will continually offer that same grace and forgiveness?" I love how Paul refused to sugarcoat his answer: "By no means." Or, in modern English, "Absolutely not!" Then he continued, "Don't you know that when you offer yourselves to someone as obedient slaves, you are slaves of the one you obey? (Romans 6:15-18)

Who or what are you obeying and serving today? Are you living in secrecy and darkness, or are you living in the light? Are you a slave to sin, or are you a slave to obedience and righteousness? The darkness may look freeing at first, but it comes with a mental and physical toll to pay. In addition, it fractures our relationship with God. Your secret could be a bottle or a pill, unhealthy food, a toxic relationship, or a computer screen. When you dabble in the wrong thing, at some point it takes over, zaps your strength, and keeps you from being the man or woman of God you were created to be. It weakens your resistance and leads to wildfires and ruin.

While discussing going outside of our proper boundaries and dabbling in forbidden things, I'd be remiss not to mention Sampson. He was a guy who had it all—looks, favor, and strength. God's power worked through him in incredible ways—snapping thick ropes, ripping down and carrying off city gates, and fending off a troop of enemy soldiers with a jawbone of a donkey, just to name a few. Yet Sampson liked to dabble in things he shouldn't, such as dating Philistine women, the idol-worshiping enemies of the

Israelites. He thought he had everything under control, that he could handle things others couldn't because he was strong and had God on his side.

If you grew up going to Sunday School, you know the rest of the story. Sampson unwisely revealed the secret of his strength—the fact that his hair had never been cut. Delilah seduced him with her beauty and flattering words. Unlike Joseph when enticed by Potiphar's wife (Genesis 39), Samson didn't flee. After all, he was Samson! He confidently fell asleep in Delilah's lap as the enemy sneaked in, clipped his locks, and tied him up. He awoke thinking he could just snap his ropes like before, but unbeknownst to Sampson, the Holy Spirit had left him, taking his supernatural strength. The enemy poked out Sampson's eyes and he had to be led around like a whipped puppy.

That's what the enemy wants to do to you. He wants to take your strength, bind you, and make you feel absolutely helpless. We'll look at the rest of Sampson's story of redemption in the next chapter, but the point now is to not be deceived. Dabbling in the wrong things will eventually get you.

It may seem that I'm only addressing men here, but be assured that women dabble too . . . and have similar consequences. It never pays to give emotional strength to a fantasy that never satisfies, that pulls you away from God's best, and can burst out of control when you least expect it.

DESTRUCTIVE PATTERNS

In the last chapter we saw that David had an undivided heart . . . for most of his life. But David was human and made mistakes. For example rather than going off to war with his men one year, he decided to stay home. He took his eyes off his God-given assignment of leadership, and he got distracted . . . by a gorgeous woman whom he happened to see bathing as he looked out of his palace. And distractions lead to dabbling. When distracted, your mind gets off focus and you become tempted by things to dabble in. Rather than diverting his eyes from the distraction and back to God, David initiated an affair with the woman, Bathsheba, who was married to one of his most valiant soldiers. The affair resulted in a pregnancy, which he did everything in his power to cover up. When nothing else worked, David arranged to have her husband die in battle (2 Samuel 11).

Satan loves nothing more than to get our attention with an attractive lure, something seemingly secret and undiscoverable to dabble in. Then, if he can just get us to go for the bait, he's got us. We're hooked and can't free ourselves. Too late, we discover that the thrill of the distraction is short-lived, but the misery that results is lasting and painful. David confessed and repented, but the consequences of his sin were set by God and delivered by Nathan the prophet: "Why did you despise the word of the Lord by doing what is evil in his eyes? You struck down Uriah the Hittite with the sword and took his wife to be your own. You killed him with the sword of the Ammonites. Now, therefore, the sword will never depart from your house" (2 Samuel 12:9-10). From that point on, the behavior of David's children brought him much pain, grief, and suffering.

The enemy knows your weakest flanks and will tempt you in the most hard-to-resist ways. He will use anything and everything to grab your attention. Some advice my dad always instilled in me was, "Zach, you've got to pay attention to what you're paying attention to." If the things of this world are always grabbing your attention, then that's what you're going to sink your teeth into. It's like taking the first bite of a big juicy burger and immediately wanting more. But if you're paying attention to the ways of the

Lord as He instructs, that's when you'll start dwelling in His presence and peace instead of dabbling.

The author of Hebrews sets a challenge before us: "Let us throw off everything that hinders and the sin that so easily entangles. And let us run with perseverance the race marked out for us, fixing our eyes on Jesus, the pioneer and perfecter of faith" (Hebrews 12:1-2). The way we avoid being sidetracked by distractions is by keeping our eyes fixed on Jesus. If we don't start there, we often find ourselves trying to deal with deadly dabbling by gritting our teeth and applying willpower . . . and we simply can't do it in our own power.

The way to avoid harmful dabbling is by establishing an authentic relationship with Jesus and experiencing His presence in our lives. "Remain in me," Jesus said, "as I also remain in you. No branch can bear fruit by itself; it must remain in the vine. Neither can you bear fruit unless you remain in me. I am the vine; you are the branches. If you remain in me and I in you, you will bear much fruit; apart from me you can do nothing" (John 15:4-5).

What kind of fruit results from remaining in the vine? The fruit of God's Spirit is "love, joy, peace, patience, kindness, goodness, faithfulness, gentleness, and self-control" (Galatians 5:22-23 ESV). And after all, isn't that what we are all looking for? If you want true life and fulfilment, stop dabbling and learn to abide in Him. That's the essence of being built different.

FIVE

DISAPPOINTED, DISCOURAGED, AND DISENGAGED

"To see ourselves as we truly are, with all our selfishness and carnality, would be devastating were it not for the grace of God that shows us what we are destined to be in Him."

— **Richard Exley**

When the Spirit of God spoke to John during one church service, he was the first at the altar. He cried out to God, laying out his dissatisfaction with his current life and a desire for a new start. From that point, he was strong, gung-ho, on target like a straight and steady arrow destined for the bull's-eye. He did the Bible studies, read the books, and went to the seminars, all of which energized him. Something was happening, something real. John felt changed, new, restored. Life was good. But then . . .

He failed, as he returned to one of his old sinful habits. And then he failed again. And again. John felt awful because he knew God must be displeased, and he was letting down his loved ones.

But he was his own worst critic as his continual sense of shame and guilt intensified. He felt like a hypocrite, thinking, *I blew it. God surely can't love someone like me, with all these secrets. Nobody else knows my struggle, pain, and desperation.*

If John only knew how many other new believers go through the same (or a very similar) struggle, he might give himself a break . . . because God certainly offers grace. But we tend to isolate ourselves when we commit to a higher standard of living and then fail to maintain it. We first become *disappointed* . . . in ourselves . . . in life . . . and in God. We think, *It felt so good for a while, but it didn't last. What's the use in even trying again?*

Then, if we allow the disappointment to take root, *discouragement* soon sets in. The two are closely related, yet miles apart. Disappointment is a letdown from unmet expectations, while discouragement is a more pervasive loss of hope. It's when the determination to move forward dies.

When that happens, the enemy finally has us where he wants us, and we simply *disengage.* Nothing pleases him more because we are no longer a threat. Instead of advancing in our spiritual growth, we become stagnant. What happens to water when it becomes stagnant? It stops flowing, loses its freshness, and becomes a breeding ground for parasites, mold, and bacteria. Often, the change goes unnoticed for a while. Imagine you're hiking in the high mountains on a hot day. You're thirsty, but you've drunk all the water in your canteen. To your delight and relief, however, you see what appears to be a spring in the distance. You run to it and drop to your knees to splash it on your face and then take a big gulp. To your horror, the water is lukewarm and smelly. Spitting it out, you realize you're not at a spring at all, but a stagnant hole!

When fresh water stops flowing, it becomes stagnant; it doesn't start out that way. Not only does stagnant water retain and grow unwanted pollutants, but it also becomes lukewarm. Nobody enjoys lukewarm water. We spit it out. It was exactly the image that Jesus used to express His distaste for the church in Laodicea: "Because you are lukewarm—neither hot nor cold—I am about to spit you out of my mouth" (Revelation 3:16). Lukewarm water was a symbol for spiritual indecision. We don't have the heat, the fire of passion, to fuel our ongoing development, but we don't want to give up completely, so we settle for a life of spiritual mediocrity. When living disengaged, we become stagnant and lukewarm, virtually useless. It's not fulfilling, and it doesn't enable us to pursue our purpose.

Perhaps the biggest reason for becoming stagnant and lukewarm is that we have failed so often that we just give up. The disappointment, discouragement, and disengagement become too entrenched. But there is a remedy for stagnant and lukewarm water: clear up what is causing the blockage and create a new flow. As a new supply of fresh water gushes forth, it washes away the stagnant and replenishes it with pure, clean liquid. In Scripture, receiving God's refreshing and abundant grace is connected to repentance (Acts 3:19-21). Charles Spurgeon expressed this eloquently:

> Our Lord Jesus is ever giving, and does not for a solitary instant withdraw his hand . . . ever sending out streams of life from his smitten side; the rain of his grace is always dropping; the river of his bounty is ever-flowing, and the well-spring of his love is constantly overflowing.[14]

POTENTIAL ALWAYS AWAITS

We began the story of Samson in the previous chapter, and I promised to follow up with the ending in this one. We left him disappointed, discouraged, and disengaged because he had lost his strength after his hair was cut. He didn't realize the real source of his strength wasn't his hair, but the Spirit of God. He had been blinded and humiliated by the Philistines who had put him to work grinding grain in prison.

But the hair on his head began to grow again. As it did, Sampson realized his folly and repented. He and God communed again. Matthew Henry noted: "Samson's afflictions were the means of bringing him to deep repentance. By the loss of his bodily sight the eyes of his understanding were opened; and by depriving him of bodily strength, the Lord was pleased to renew his spiritual strength."[15]

When Samson heard that all the Philistine rulers were going to assemble to praise their god Dagon for his capture, he saw an opportunity. When the day came, Samson cried out to God for one more display of strength, and his prayer was answered. God empowered Samson to take out the pillars that held up their temple, and more Philistines died that day than Samson had destroyed throughout his lifetime (Judges 16:23-31).

In the annals of Israel's history, Samson is remembered as one of their heroes of the faith, and is even included in the "Faith Hall of Fame" in Hebrews 11 (v. 32). As we previously noted, he dabbled in some serious distractions during his lifetime and wasn't exactly a shining example of godly behavior, but then, most of the other names on that list in Hebrews had their own serious shortcomings. They were all flawed human beings, but they kept living for God because they were built different. Awareness of that fact should bring us hope.

God never deserted Samson, and He will never desert you either. You may have lost a lot of time and resources in meaningless pursuits, but God specializes in redeeming the past. He may correct your situation, or he may offer you a brand new start, but the sooner you choose to reengage, the sooner He can shower you with His healing and refreshing love.

If you get out of sync with God, simply keep coming back to Jesus—ten times, a hundred times, a thousand times, it doesn't matter. God doesn't want to shame you; He wants to free you. Every time you fail and are restored to God's good graces, you should love Jesus a little more. The song "Amazing Grace" gets sweeter, and worship becomes much richer when you realize His grace is unlimited . . . and always available to you.

We all need grace, and grace is available to us all. Paul makes both points very clearly: "All have sinned and fall short of the glory of God, and all are justified freely by his grace through the redemption that came by Christ Jesus" (Romans 3:23-24). None of the principles in this book work unless they are applied in the framework of grace. Without understanding and applying grace, everything we've talked about is hollow and meaningless.

Here's what happens to the true believer who possesses the Holy Spirit. Each time we fall and get up, the stronger we get, and the more we become like Jesus. Pastor and radio host Steve Brown writes:

> You may not know it, but unbelievably rich spiritual power is available to you. This spiritual power is not the result of being more religious, acquiring more knowledge about God, moving to a monastery, being more obedient, or praying more often. I suppose there is nothing wrong with those things, but they don't yield spiritual power. The source of spiritual power is repentance . . . Repentance isn't changing; it's God's way of changing us . . . Repentance is a source of great power, but only if you know you need to repent.[16]

We don't excuse sin, we strive for holiness. But when we fall, we fall at the foot of the Cross, and Jesus picks us up every time . . . every single time. It's a supernatural thing.

Brennan Manning wrote this incredible piece that I believe applies to most of us:

In the arc of my unremarkable life, wherein the victories have been small and personal, the trials fairly pedestrian, and the failures large enough to deeply wound me and those I love, I have repeated endlessly the pattern of falling down and getting up, falling down and getting up. Each time I fall, I am propelled to renew my efforts by a blind trust in the forgiveness of my sins from sheer grace, in the acquittal, vindication, and justification of my ragged journey based not on any good deeds I have done (the approach taken by the Pharisee in the temple) but on an unflagging trust in the love of a gracious and merciful God.[17]

One of the psalms of David expresses it this way:

The Lord is compassionate and gracious,
slow to anger, abounding in love.
He will not always accuse,
nor will he harbor his anger forever;
he does not treat us as our sins deserve,
or repay us according to our iniquities.
For as high as the heavens are above the earth,
so great is his love for those who fear him;
as far as the east is from the west,
so far has he removed our transgressions from us.
(Psalm 103:8-12)

Edwin Louis Cole has been heralded "the father of the Christian men's movement." He writes: "If God forgives us, but we do not forgive ourselves, we make ourselves greater than Him. Wisely forgetting the past is part of man's maturing."[18] (I would add this is true for women too!)

Peace comes from the Lord when we trust in His promises and provision for our sins and failures. Not only does your role here and what you do matter, *you* matter. Even if, like Samson, you have failed and find yourself grinding grain for people you detest, God wants to bring you out of the depths of discouragement and disengagement. He wants to reengage you and give you a new enthusiasm for life.

My prayer is that the remainder of this book will encourage and equip you with some life-giving and perspective-shifting principles to help you step out of the pit and into the purpose God has called you to.

SIX

WHAT ARE YOU FIGHTING FOR?

"There is no other man [or woman] who can replace
you in your life, in the arena you've been called to.
If you leave your place in the line, it will remain empty.
No one else can be who you are meant to be.
You are the hero in your story."

— **John Eldredge**

ndiana resident David Miller was driving a dump truck when he was forced off the road by an out-of-control car. His truck swerved into a ditch, crashed head-on into a utility pole, flipped over, and burst into flames. The dramatic accident caused quite a commotion as people immediately gathered and began staring at the burning truck. Meanwhile, Miller was desperate to escape, but his foot had gotten wedged between the clutch and the floorboard. As he screamed for help and wrestled to get free, the group of onlookers just stood by, too afraid to go near the flames.

A man named Tim Vachon drove upon the scene and saw the crowd paralyzed there, unable or unwilling to help. Refusing to stand idly by and watch, Tim took off running toward the flaming dump truck. It was his instinct—and a mark of his character—to try to save the driver. Tim didn't ponder the danger, only the needs of a desperate man trapped inside his vehicle.

At first, the searing heat kept Tim back because the door was bent and wouldn't open. At that point, Miller managed to kick out the window from inside with his free foot, enabling Tim to unwedge Miller's foot and pull him out of the burning truck with only moments to spare. Tim credits God for putting him in the right place at the right time. As for David Miller, he's incredibly grateful that Tim had the courage to step up when no one else would.

Things were so hectic on the day of the fiery crash that Tim and David never really got a chance to talk, so the two reunited a few days after the accident. David hugged Tim and thanked him for bravely coming to his rescue when no one else would. David's wife, Trudy, came along for the reunion. She also wanted to thank the man responsible for keeping her husband alive. She started crying when she saw Tim. "It didn't really hit me until this morning that our anniversary is next week," Trudy said. "So, I don't really know what an anniversary would be like without my husband."

"I cried when I left the scene," David said. "I realized God kept us safe through it all because . . . that fire just took over that quick. And I thanked God and Tim."[19]

NOT BOUND BY TIME

Did you know that God determined for you to live in this exact time and place in history? According to Acts 17:26, "From one man [God] made all the nations, that they should inhabit the whole earth; and he marked out their appointed times in history and the boundaries of their lands." In my opinion, that is one of the most amazing Scriptures in the Bible. Do you believe it? *Can* you believe it? If you can, it will change your whole perspective.

You weren't just a random thought or accident. God is even bigger than time itself. He created time and knows everything—past, present, and future. Jesus, God in the flesh, knew the rooster was going to crow immediately after Peter denied Him the third time (Matthew 26:34). When preparing for His last supper, He knew a donkey would be tied up and waiting (Luke 19:30).

He also knows everything about you, and He has put you in this specific moment and place in time for a purpose. To begin with, He puts you where you are most likely to seek and find Him (Isaiah 55:60). And then, He has a specific assignment that only you can complete. It may be to reach and impact one person or perhaps your entire circle of influence.

However, not everyone is quick to acknowledge God's plan and presence. In fact, most don't. They are content to wait, to stall, to stand by rubbernecking while people are dying around them. But somebody out there is waiting for you to move. It could be a friend, your children, grandchildren, spouse, or someone trapped in a life circumstance. You've been given specific gifts needed by those in your life. Without your voice and influence, there's a vacancy that no one else can replace. It's your moment. Will you be ready, or will you let it pass you by?

A GREATER PURPOSE

John Maxwell connects success in life with finding your purpose. He writes:

> Over the years as I have watched and listened to successful people, I have discovered a common thread: They know why they're here. Knowing their purpose in life gives them

stability. And when others around them start abandoning their causes and jumping ship when life gets tough, these people use this assurance to steady the boat, to ride out the storm because they have a true North Star. It becomes an anchor in their life—a confidence based upon knowledge of purpose. Someone once said there are two great days in life—the day you are born and the day you discover why. I'm here to tell you that highly successful people have discovered why.[20]

The 2005 movie, *Cinderella Man*, was inspired by the true story of boxer Jimmy Braddock (played by Russell Crowe). During the Great Depression of the 1930s, Braddock made an unlikely comeback to challenge for the heavyweight championship of the world. Many saw him as a washed-up, mediocre has-been. In one scene, Braddock is preparing to fight the #1 heavyweight champion of the world, Max Baer, who had already killed three men in the ring. Jimmy's wife and family were terrified for his life and pleaded with him to call off what they feared was an almost certain death sentence, but Braddock wouldn't back down. When he and his wife were being interviewed at the pre-fight press conference, a reporter asked him why he believed he could win. Jimmy shouted back, "This time around I know what I'm fighting for."

"What's that, Jimmy?" asked the reporter.

"I fight for milk."[21]

Jimmy Braddock was fighting for something greater than himself. The fight was no longer for a Championship belt or prestige or fame. It was for his family.

What are you fighting for? What's your purpose? We all have a calling that's more than merely a dream. Your purpose is what pushes you through the days when you don't feel like doing what you initially set out to do. Friedrich Nietzsche once said, "He who has a why to live for can bear almost any how." Knowing and understanding your why—your purpose—is essential.

A modern-day definition of *tragedy* is "being successful in things that really don't matter." It's easy to get lost and confused in life. When people can't find their zone or their lane in life, they get lost and start reaching for things that don't satisfy and don't last. You'll see a clear difference in those who are strong of heart. They lead with purpose, climb the mountains, and run into the storms. They are wired differently. They're built different.

All the men and women I know who are truly built different are rooted in a greater purpose, a greater vision, a greater meaning, and a greater reason than themselves. Consider the many heroes of the Bible who lived with a purpose that they were willing to fight for—to die for—a purpose that was greater than themselves. What if Esther hadn't wielded her influence before King Xerxes? An entire people group would have been eliminated. What if Joseph had allowed the disappointing events of his life to keep him from discovering God's purpose for him? All of Egypt and many other nations would have starved. What if Rahab hadn't risked all to hide the Israelite spies at Jericho? What if Moses' mother hadn't defied Pharaoh's command to kill her child? What if David hadn't stepped out from the crowd and made his stand against Goliath? What if Nehemiah hadn't overcome intense resistance to rebuild the walls of Jerusalem? The list goes on and on. All their decisions to take a stand for God required an element of risk, yet the futures of individuals, families, and nations were enriched because of their actions.

Some people justify their inaction by saying, "I'm waiting for God to act," but it may be that He's waiting for them to get moving. It's true that Isaiah wrote, "They who wait for the Lord shall renew their strength; they shall mount up with wings like eagles; they shall run and not be weary; they shall walk and not faint" (Isaiah 40:31 ESV). The words "wait for" here don't mean to sit and do nothing. It's not a passive, indifferent biding of time. This sense of biblical waiting is active anticipation that, given time, God is going to act.

Sometimes the best thing we can do is be still before the Lord and listen for His voice and direction, but many times He supplies the strength needed beyond ourselves while we are moving! God responds to faith. Sometimes faith means staying put. Other times it means getting moving.

The exciting thing about responding to God's call to action is that you never know where it will take you. Abraham left the comfort of his homeland without question, and God gave him an unexpected family, land, and a legacy. Peter obeyed and found himself walking on the water with Jesus. Let's all listen carefully for God's leading, and then look with eager expectation for whatever He would have us do, wherever He would have us go.

SEVEN

RELEASING YOUR INNER BEAST

"You can't just turn into a beast;
you already have to be the beast!"

— Inky Johnson

nky Johnson was a defensive back at the University of Tennessee whom the scouting experts were projecting to be a first-round pick in the 2007 NFL draft. After an impressive first game of his senior year, Tennessee faced off against Air Force. Late in the second half of that hard-fought game, Inky made a routine tackle on the sideline. Little did he know it would be the last hit he'd ever make on a football field. Something happened during that tackle that caused Inky's entire right arm, from his shoulder to his hand, to become permanently paralyzed. He would never play football again.

Inky's life was forever altered. Surely he must have struggled with thoughts of despair and depression. Football had been such a large component of his identity, and now it was gone. Now what? What was he made of? What was in his core?

But Inky was no stranger to challenge and hardship. He grew up in a single parent, two-bedroom home housing fourteen people. His mom worked double shifts every night to make ends meet. Many people would likely have developed a victim mentality, yet even in the harshest of circumstances, Inky Johnson always found a way to be grateful. After a lot of self-examination following his football injury, Inky now inspires millions with his story of overcoming adversity and adapting to change.[22] In addition, he has developed programs to help mentor underprivileged youth around the country. One of his guiding principles is, "How you view what you do is how you do what you do."[23]

WHEN THE PRESSURE IS ON

Extreme pressure can crush rocks, but it can also produce diamonds. About 100 miles below the Earth's mantle, under conditions of intense pressure (about 725,000 pounds per square inch) and heat (2,000 degrees Fahrenheit), carbon atoms bond and crystallize, forming diamonds. If the carbon isn't present, no diamond forms. Carbon is the "it factor."

Life has its own way of creating intense pressure and turning up the heat to uncomfortable temperatures. Just as with the diamond in the rough, the heat and pressure of life don't just help mold us; they reveal us. Whoever we are deep in our core either crystallizes into something stronger, or it gets crushed. Second-century Greek philosopher Epictetus said, "Circumstances don't make the man, they only reveal him to himself." He should know. He was born into slavery before getting an education and becoming an esteemed philosopher.

My dad said it this way: "Pressure or adversity expose who you are." My grandmother would say, "What's in the well, comes up in the bucket." Pain and adversity will inevitably come, and during the heat of the battle, some people step up while others run away. Some fold, while others rise. Some cower in fear, while others rumble with joy.

I've always been fascinated by the great sports figures and elite athletes who thrive in do-or-die situations. Sometimes they prevail when everyone is rooting against them, but I'm especially impressed by the ones who sustain their success time after time when everyone is counting on them to come through with the victory. It's during those crunch-time situations that they take their game to a whole new level. They become more focused and more dialed in, and they shine when everything is on the line. Some would call this a killer instinct, but Seattle Seahawks running back Marshawn Lynch calls it "Beast Mode"—a phrase that became his official nickname.

Many ask the question, "Other than raw talent, what's the deciding factor between exceptional athletes and mediocre ones?" I've been fortunate to have had the opportunity of walking alongside and interviewing several of the most elite and decorated athletes, military heroes, ministry leaders, and successful business professionals in our world today. I've studied and observed what separates them from the rest in terms of remaining resilient and mentally tough in the face of extreme pressure and adversity, and one of the biggest keys in unlocking their full potential is *reshaping their perspective*. Like carbon is the "it factor" for a diamond, perspective is the "it factor" for humans.

PERSPECTIVE STEERS POTENTIAL

My family, closest friends, and teammates could tell you that as I was growing up, I struggled terribly with performance anxiety. The intense fear of failure and unmet expectations nagged me, and I hated the thought of disappointing others. It got so bad that I began experiencing the somatic symptoms of nausea before nearly every game. The weird thing was, it only affected me *leading up to* the game. Once the game started, I was fine. But one day I ended up "getting sick" in front of all my teammates and coaching staff during our pregame speech. I felt so deflated, embarrassed, and tired of wrestling this fear and worry that I went to my dad and asked him if there was anything I could start doing before games to calm or soothe me. I think that was the first of many times he told me to "Start paying attention to what you're paying attention to." Start focusing on seeing yourself having success, making plays, hitting the ball hard—having fun with your friends.

The mind can be a beautifully creative and free place, but it can also be a painful, turbulent, prison *if we let it.* We get out of life what we *look for* in it. Over time, I began reshaping my perspective to acknowledge that my expectation is what fuels my effort and execution in this life.

Those who are built different have learned (or are learning) the art of using pain as a motivation to rise higher and move forward with resolve. Pain, adversity, challenge, and failure become fuel for their fire. Pain can hold you in bondage if you allow it to, or you can channel it to become your passport to take you places you would never have been able to go without it. Yes, it's hard. It is uncomfortable. No one is denying that. But you can choose to allow it to produce something good in your life if you determine to do so.

Life may have beaten you down to your knees, and you're struggling to get back up. You just can't seem to rise above the challenge and struggle you're currently facing. But you can get up off the canvas and engage! Take the advice of the Apostle James: "Consider it pure joy, my brothers and sisters, whenever you face trials of many kinds, because you know the testing of your faith produces perseverance. Let perseverance finish its work so that you may be mature and complete, not lacking anything" (James

1:2-4). In modern vernacular, that means, "Even when life stinks, consider it a great joy—not because of the circumstances you find yourself in, but because of what those circumstances can and will produce within you if you choose to have the right perspective." Embracing the reality that God wants to use the challenges and difficulties we experience in this life for our good is truly a gift that we can view with joy.

I believe the elements to create meaningful moments are inside us all, but they tend to remain stagnant in hibernation until they are jarred awake. Sometimes just the right "cause" or "pressure" awakens your sleeping potential, but ultimately it's your perspective that determines if it's awakened or not. Interestingly, although most people view pressure through the lens of fear and worry, I've come to realize that those who find real peace during challenge and adversity have chosen the following unique perspective.

PRESSURE IS A PRIVILEGE

Tim Grover, arguably one of the greatest trainers of all time, has trained athletes including Michael Jordan, Kobe Bryant, Dwayne Wade, Russell Wilson, and many more. He describes that some of the best of the best thrive under pressure because they view it as a privilege. They understand that someone believes in them, so they need to believe in themselves. Think about it in terms of sports. The reason an athlete gets called to the free throw line to shoot technical foul shots, has his number called on the final play of the game, or is brought in from the bullpen to shut things down with the team barely hanging on by a thread is because someone believes in them. Tim writes:

> Are there times when you truly have no control? Absolutely.
> But at that point, it's on you to figure out how to take charge

and navigate forward. Otherwise, you're allowing external pressure to dictate the outcome. Create your own pressure to succeed, don't allow others to create it for you. Have the confidence to trust that you can handle anything.[24]

When we are going through painful seasons in our lives, what if we didn't ask God *why*? What if, instead, we had the perspective that God *chose* us to walk through this valley, desert, or fiery furnace in life. If we believe that, we know He will surely walk alongside us through it. And we *should* be confident that God believes in us. He says:

> **"Do not fear, for I have redeemed you; I have summoned you by name; you are mine. When you pass through the waters, I will be with you; and when you pass through the rivers, they will not sweep over you. When you walk through the fire, you will not be burned, the flames will not set you ablaze."**
> **(Isaiah 43:1-2)**

There's peace and confident expectation that comes in knowing *who* you are by first remembering *whose* you are.

Joan of Arc is an awe-inspiring example of this principle. She was most definitely built different. Though a common medieval peasant girl, when she felt the heat and the pressure, a diamond was created and a beast was unleashed. Joan served an extraordinary God and had an extraordinary relationship with Him.

God had been speaking to Joan for a while. As the plight of France worsened during their conflict with England during the Hundred Years' War, the intensity of her prayers increased. God answered her cries by giving her a vision and an assignment. The city of Orleans had been under siege for months and Joan felt part of her divine assignment was to rally a group of soldiers from the Royal Army and lead them into battle to free the city—an extremely bold vision for a farm girl in a wool tunic and pigtails. Who would have thought that God would use a simple farmer's daughter as a mighty military warrior leading a brigade of the French Royal army into battle to begin freeing their nation?

The king eventually (and surprisingly) granted Joan's request for soldiers. While the troops were being pulled together for this very difficult mission, Joan took a quick lesson in military fighting and was fitted for armor. News of Joan's vision from God and the king's sanction reached Orleans before she did, causing hope among the people. During the heat of the battle, an arrow pierced Joan's neck. She pulled it out quickly, had the wound dressed, and returned to the fight. After the dust settled, the English had been driven out and the city of Orleans was once again free. Over the next two months, Joan led the French army in several more memorable victories.

Later, Joan was captured by England. After being wrongly convicted of witchcraft, she was burned alive at the stake. Witnesses claimed that as the flames engulfed her, Joan sang praises to God and asked for a cross to be held in front of her face as she called out to Jesus. Ultimately, Joan of Arc was exonerated of all charges and officially canonized as a saint in 1920. Charles Spurgeon, known as the prince of preachers (and who, by the way, was from England), had this to say about Joan of Arc:

> Do not talk to me about Joan of Arc! This is the true heroine. She is battling with death and singing while she dies. Fear? She has long forgotten what that means. Doubt? It is banished. Distress? Despondency? She has left them all behind. She is a believer; she has received Jesus, and she has power

to be a child of God. Oh, the honor and dignity of being born from above![25]

Real life is no playground; it's a *battleground*. As we have seen, physical bodies get paralyzed, countries get invaded, and worse. Relationships are at stake: the souls of our families, friends, fellow believers, and our own connection with God. We have a very real enemy of our souls that isn't playing around. So, when the inevitable pain arises, adversity hits, pressure swells, and your moment comes, you can't just turn into the beast. You already have to be the beast!

Your perspective will always drive your potential.

EIGHT

YOU CAN'T WARM UP TO PLAY!

"Show me your habits, I'll show you your future."
— Mark Batterson

A few years back, I had the honor of accompanying my dad when he was asked to share at the Pittsburgh Steelers team chapel before their big AFC-North showdown with the Baltimore Ravens. It was a winner-take-all game. Whoever won, took the division. The Saturday night before the game, we got to sit in on a team meeting in the hotel. All the players had just come in from their pregame practice. Everybody was chit-chatting around, but a hush dropped over the room the moment Coach Tomlin stepped in. He didn't say a word. He didn't have to. You could feel the weight of his authority as he walked down the aisle to the front. He turned, surveyed his team, locked eyes with them, and began shouting, "You can't warm up to play! You can't warm up to play! You can't warm up to play!" Then he launched into his heartfelt pregame speech. It was so motivational it made me want to jump up and run through the hotel walls! To this day, I still can't get those words out of my head. "You can't warm up to play!"

The next morning the team would walk out onto the field, go through their warmup routine, then buckle their chin straps and line up for the kickoff. Obviously, Coach Tomlin wasn't saying that warming up isn't important. What he was saying is, when that opening whistle blows, it's too late to warm up. If you expect to compete and win, you'd better hit it full-speed, fully engaged. No second-guessing or simply going through the motions like in warmups. Oh, technically you *can* just go through the motions during the game, but if you do, you'll get your head handed to you! You can't expect to win if you aren't fully engaged in the moment.

The Apostle Paul put it this way: "Do you not know that in a race all the runners run, but only one gets the prize? Run in such a way as to get the prize" (1 Corinthians 9:24). Anybody can run in a race, but only one gets the prize. Some just run lackadaisically. Some settle for mediocrity—less than their best. But in your walk with God, being lackadaisical won't work if you expect to receive what God has for you. You won't be ready to step into your divine moments if you aren't fully engaged and prepared. The athletes who win are built different. So are the Christians who receive what God has for them.

PREPARATION = SEPARATION

One way we run to win the prize is to commit to intense training and preparation *before* the race. Lionel Messi, who some dub as the best soccer player in the world, said, "It took me years to become an overnight success." Michael Jordan once said, "It's what happens in empty gymnasiums that fills arenas."

What are you doing when no one's watching? Are the steps you're taking today—both publicly and privately—pushing you closer or pulling you farther away from your goals? Goals, dreams, and aspirations are great, but there's not a championship athlete out there who competes at the top levels and wins without years of hard work.

Just. Doesn't. Happen.

What separates winners from the others is often preparation. Preparation equals separation. You can't warm up to play, and you can't play to win without proper preparation. Paul had more to say about that:

> Everyone who competes in the games goes into strict training. They do it to get a crown that will not last, but we do it to get a crown that will last forever. Therefore I do not run like someone running aimlessly; I do not fight like a boxer beating the air. No, I strike a blow to my body and make it my slave so that after I have preached to others, I myself will not be disqualified for the prize.
> (1 Corinthians 9:25-27)

Those are some heavy-duty words. Paul is saying that he would never run this Christian race lackadaisically. He prepares himself by going into strict training, including (as he switches to a boxing analogy) bringing his physical body under subjection. Like him, I want all God has for me—the prize here on earth that comes from knowing and obeying Him, and the rewards that await the obedient in heaven. To be built different and strive to be all He wants me to be takes disciplined training while developing spiritual habits.

It's critical to understand that I'm not talking about flexing our muscles and exerting our willpower, determining to grind out this Christian life. That will never work and only leads to failure and frustration. Richard Foster calls this "will worship." In his classic book, *Celebration of Discipline*, He writes:

Will worship may produce an outward show of success for a time, but in the cracks and crevices of our lives our deep inner condition will eventually be revealed. Jesus describes this condition when he speaks of the external righteousness of the Pharisees. . . . Inner righteousness is a gift from God to be graciously received. The needed change within us is God's work, not ours. . . . We cannot attain or earn this righteousness of the kingdom of God; it is a grace that is given. . . . God has given us the Disciplines of the spiritual life as a means of receiving his grace. The Disciplines allow us to place ourselves before God so that he can transform us. [26]

We are saved by grace and maintained by God's grace, and that is the only way to achieve the righteousness of God. But that's just the first step in being built different. Salvation is free and open to all, but as we build more effective and productive relationships with God and others, we need to put some work into "the Disciplines" (that Foster listed as meditation, prayer, study, submission, service, confession, worship, celebration, and others). Doing so can change our lives in ways we can't even imagine.

As I was pondering Foster's quote, a passage from 2 Peter came ringing to my mind. It's incredibly significant to this chapter and to being built different. Keep in mind that Peter is addressing those who are already believers.

To those who through the righteousness of our God and Savior Jesus Christ have received faith as precious as ours:

Grace and peace be yours in abundance through the knowledge of God and of Jesus our Lord.

His divine power has given us everything we need for a godly life through our knowledge of him who called us by his own glory and goodness. Through these he has given us his very great and precious promises, so that through them you may participate in the divine nature, having escaped the corruption in the world caused by evil desires.

For this very reason, make every effort to add to your faith goodness; and to goodness, knowledge; and to knowledge, self-control; and to self-control, perseverance; and to perseverance, godliness; and to godliness, mutual affection; and to mutual affection, love. For if you possess these qualities in increasing measure, they will keep you from being ineffective and unproductive in your knowledge of our Lord Jesus Christ. But whoever does not have them is nearsighted and blind, forgetting that they have been cleansed from their past sins.

Therefore, my brothers and sisters, make every effort to confirm your calling and election. For if you do these things, you will never stumble, and you will receive a rich welcome into the eternal kingdom of our Lord and Savior Jesus Christ. (2 Peter 1:1-11)

More than once in that passage Peter challenges us to "make every effort" to build on the salvation and faith that God supplies so freely. And as I review the list of qualities we should learn to display as believers, I am reminded of a lesson I learned in college.

As a boy I had dreamed of one day playing Division 1 baseball and then having a shot to play in the big leagues—MLB. One of the happiest days of my life was when I signed to play for Liberty University in my hometown of Lynchburg, Virginia. When I graduated from high school, I had been selected Varsity Team Capitan, MVP, All-State, All-Conference, Division 1 VISAA Player of the

Year, and more. At the first team meeting at Liberty where the Freshmen recruits would be introduced to the veterans, I walked in flying high, on top of the world. I had "the stuff" . . . or so I thought.

Jim Toman was Liberty's head baseball coach at the time. He said, "Hey, everybody. Welcome back to the new year. Welcome our new recruits. Before we get started, I just want everyone to know a little bit more about the other individuals in the room. Please stand up if you were team MVP of your high school baseball team." I stood and puffed my chest out a little, thinking I was special . . . and saw that everybody in the room was standing.

"Okay, sit down," Coach Toman said. "Now, I want everybody who was First Team All Conference—not second or third—please rise." Again, I stood . . . also with everyone else. I was starting to get the message.

"All right, boys, sit back down. Now everybody that was First Team All-State stand." Again, the whole team stood up, which just humbled me and all the new guys. Coach looked at us and said, "If you boys haven't noticed, every guy in this room is talented. Now here's the deal. There's going to be a *defining factor* that separates the men from the boys, and it's your job to figure out what that is."

I've never forgotten that, and it didn't take me long to discover what the *defining factor* is, at least, a critical part. It's not who's most talented. It's not who's the biggest or the fastest. Though talent matters, the separation is in the preparation—those who succeed are the ones who are willing to work their hardest in the weight room, at pitchers' practice drills, fielding ground balls and bunts, sprints, batting practice, and learning to function at both the right consistency and the right intensity. When we focus on those basic elements, we develop the intangibles that make all the difference in a big game . . . and in life. Character, perseverance, integrity, humility, persistence, leadership, work ethic, and heart are the disciplines for athletes, and many of those qualities are the same as the ones Peter listed for believers determined to grow in their faith. It's standing out in those little ways, which are not little at all, that enable us to function when the pressure is on, or when facing a powerful opponent.

"It's not the will to win that matters," said the great Paul "Bear" Bryant. "Everyone has that. It's the will to prepare to win that matters." And many motivational speakers today borrow from the ancient Greek poet Archilochus to remind their listeners that, "We don't rise to the level of our expectations; we fall to the level of our training."[27] That one's worth writing down and sticking on your bathroom mirror.

A seminary professor told his class the week before the final exam, "There are rare occasions when God performs miracles. However, most of the time, if you pray for an A but only study for a D, you can expect to get a D."

Expectation is useless without proper preparation. The unforeseen trials we face often reveal unanticipated "God moments" where we have opportunities to display our faith and see Him work in wonderful ways . . . if we're prepared. Have we been paying attention to His promises in Scripture? Do we regularly acknowledge His presence in our lives in small ways? Are we making regular efforts to love our neighbors as ourselves? If so, when the tough challenges come, perhaps a whole new level of faith will kick in, and you'll see God's love and power in surprising ways. But someone can have the heart of a diamond in their core, but it will stay unrefined and rough if it is never prepared.

If physical preparation is important for elite athletes, then spiritual preparing is even more so for believers who want to receive all God has for them. The Apostle Paul challenges us to "train yourself to be godly. For physical training is of some value, but godliness has value for all things, holding promise for both the present life and the life to come. This is a trustworthy saying that deserves full acceptance" (1 Timothy 4:7-9).

PEACE COMES FROM HIS PRESENCE

At the 2021 American Association of Christian Counselors World Conference, speaker Levi Lusko left the sold-out crowd speechless. The nearly 7,000 counselors, psychologists, psychiatrists, coaches, and pastors heard him describe with great vulnerability the struggle and pain he and his family endured after the sudden and tragic loss of their daughter, Lenya, in 2012. As he shared the excruciating turmoil and disappointment he had faced, he also described the intimacy he experienced with the Lord during that period of his life. Not surprisingly, he was upset, angry, and grieving, yet he continued to *choose worship*—a lesson he'd learned from the book of Job for how to prepare for what will seem like the worst day of our lives.

As you may know, Job's story begins by describing him as a righteous man who has a deep adoration for and intimate relationship with the Lord. God himself describes Job as "blameless and upright, a man who fears God and shuns evil" (Job 1:8). Then Satan, wanting to rupture that relationship, challenged the Lord concerning Job's love, suggesting that as soon as the many blessings from God were removed, Job's love for Him would fade. In a startlingly rapid sequence, Job suffered the loss of his possessions, finances, children, and personal health. He was left sitting in an ash heap, scraping his sores with shards of broken pottery. He still had his wife, but her advice was to "Curse God and die!" (Job 2:7-10)

Yet even amid all that incredible heartbreak, poverty, discouragement, disappointment, depression, doubt, and pain, Job remained faithful (Job 1:20-22; 2:10). But where did all Job's power to stand firm in his faith come from? How did he endure and remain devoted to the Lord through all of this? Pastor Levi reminded us that the power to address the pain had already been developed. Before any of Job's terrible disasters struck, he had made it his *regular custom* to get up early in the morning, worship God, pray, and offer a sacrifice for each of his children (Job 1:5). Job was training for the trial he was not yet facing.

How do you choose to worship God when it's the worst day of your life? By making it a daily, disciplined practice to worship Him when it's *not* the worst day of your life. I'm reminded of Paul's words in Philippians 4. Even after being repeatedly imprisoned, beaten, disrespected, cursed at, and worse throughout his life for the cause of Christ, Paul's outlook was surprisingly optimistic: "Rejoice in the Lord always, I will say it again: Rejoice! Let your gentleness [confidence] be evident to all. The Lord is near" (Philippians 4:4-5).

The Apostle Paul was prepared for even the most difficult of circumstances by continually acknowledging that the Lord was near—regardless of his feelings! He *practiced the presence and power of God* in his life every single day, no matter what! The Lord is fully present in our lives as well. He is near. Understanding this truth prepares us for the battles that will inevitably come in this life.

And then Paul added: "Do not be anxious for anything" (Philippians 4:6). Even after undergoing all he went through, Paul encourages us to not be anxious. There's only one way Paul could have pulled that off: he had to know and believe that Jesus was real and present in every circumstance. We should make it a more regular habit to rejoice in the truth that God sees us and loves us. As one of my favorite worship songs says, "He doesn't lead you to leave you."

Remember, preparation is what separates the Jobs and the Pauls of life from ordinary believers. And in addition, your preparation will also fuel your expectation.

Whether you are Joan of Arc, a high school teacher, a farmer, or whatever or whoever, God has a unique plan for your life. He wants you to run to win your prize. Don't settle for less than your best. And if you want to know what you'll do when it really counts, start by looking at what you're doing when it doesn't. Anything you do consistently becomes a part of your habits and routine. So today, no matter what your circumstance, start training for the worst day of your life . . . and you'll be ready when it gets here.

NINE

DREAMING WITH YOUR CREATOR

"It is about becoming what God created you to be. . . .
You were made by God and for God—and until you
understand that, life will never make sense."
— Rick Warren

What were your dreams when you were a kid? I've shared mine: being the hero in a high-stakes athletic event, be it football, basketball, baseball, or whatever. I loved competing, and I regularly envisioned myself as the star.

Other friends wanted to be Olympics champions, Grammy-award-winning singers, famous authors, astronauts, and self-made billionaires. But the one thing we all had in common was that we wanted to be a superstar—the one who stood out—in that field. None of us ever dreamed of just being average, of "sitting on the bench" throughout life. We would never consider playing it safe when a daring heart and brave soul were needed. We wanted to slay the giant, rush into the burning house and pull the people to safety, step down the ladder of the lunar module onto the moon.

We sensed even at a young age that risk was a necessary element in personal growth and excitement in life.

So what happens to us? At what point do we quash our dreams and start settling for average . . . or for "safe"?

Michael Jordan said, "Some people want it to happen, some wish it would happen, others make it happen."[28] That much is true, but here's a word of warning: you can only make something happen if it's within your own gifts, talents, and calling. Nothing is more frustrating than trying to be the world's best oak tree when you were created to be a pine tree.

I learned this lesson during my freshman year of high school baseball. We were playing a local powerhouse school and weren't giving them much competition, so our coach decided to move me from my position on second base to try pitching. That was before I had done a lot of training and was throwing a whopping 75 mph "fastball"—not exactly "bringing the heat!" To make things worse, the bases were loaded, and their best player was coming up to bat! On the first pitch I threw, I heard the distinctive *crack* of bat on ball, and watched the ball sail over our field's tall left field fence to where I presume it got lost somewhere in the distant mall parking lot. I remember the discouragement I felt. The feeling of failure can be terribly humiliating and embarrassing.

But as I grew through my career, I realized I wasn't meant to be the next Nolan Ryan. I didn't have the power arm and electric fastball that great pitchers do. However, I had my own innate and unique abilities that I developed as a pitcher. I could throw a natural cut fastball, locate my pitches, and vary speeds to keep batters off balance. And I just flat-out loved to compete. The only reason I had the success I did pitching at both the high school and collegiate level was because I invested time in developing my craft. Instead of trying to become something or someone I was not, I tried to become the best version of myself.

No matter how much you work and prepare, you'll never excel at something you're not, so don't even try. Sometimes failure, as I just demonstrated, is the best thing that can happen to a person if it shows them what they are *not* and is used as a stepping-stone to propel them to where they need to be. Develop the mindset that you either win or you learn.

Author and motivational speaker Richard J. Needham says, "Strong people make as many and as ghastly mistakes as weak people. The difference is that strong people admit them, laugh at them, learn from them. That is how they become strong."[29] I'll add, "People whose mantra is *even if*."

Learn to embrace your uniqueness. The enemy would love for you to die trying to copy someone else instead of being the unique individual the Lord made you to be. What I mean by that is, you can live your whole life doing good things that need to be done, but never accomplish the thing(s) you were uniquely created to do. Anybody can just go through the motions of life, but the people who have the greatest impact and satisfaction are the ones who know what they are *not*. They have identified their strengths and weaknesses, and they press into their unique calling and purpose. As they apply their unique gifts and talents, doors open for them and fulfilling opportunities arise.

Those who are built different have found their zone, their lane. You can be young, just hitting adulthood, middle-aged, or elderly. Look through Scripture. God doesn't discriminate. He calls all ages to work with Him and accomplish His will in His timing. "I am sure of this," wrote Paul, "that he who began a good work in you will bring it to completion at the day of Jesus Christ" (Philippians 1:6 ESV).

God has a calling for you. It may be a new assignment, or perhaps something that you started long ago and never completed. It doesn't matter how much you may have strayed or fallen off course, you can still finish strong. God delights in taking wounded and broken people and bringing them back into alignment, molding them into powerful warriors for His causes. He loves to use our moments of powerlessness to draw us closer to Him.

Of course, it all begins by being anchored and rooted in a relationship with Christ himself. "Let your roots grow down into him," Scripture says, "and let your lives be built on him" (Colossians 2:7 NLT). Without Him we have an unstable foundation. But with Jesus as our foundation, we can become who *He* created us to be—the best version of ourselves, and different from everyone else on earth.

Why work so hard to fit in when you were born to stand out? God wants to give you a dream—a vision of what He wants to accomplish through you that is built into your personal DNA. When you find your lane, that's where your source of ultimate success and fulfilment will be.

How will you know if yours is a God-originated dream? It will not only be fulfilling for you, but will also connect you to others. God-dreams are always about impacting the lives of others through using your God-given gifts, empowered by the Holy Spirit. An often-repeated proverb says, "Where there is no vision, the people perish" (Proverbs 29:18 KJV). I believe that proverb can be interpreted a couple of ways. Certainly, when people don't have any direction from God, they are prone to wander into destructive patterns. But another way to look at it is that when *you* don't pursue your God-vision, the people you know who need what you have will suffer loss. Additionally, when you don't respond to your God-dream, your soul suffers loss. Whenever we limit what God can do through us, we (and perhaps others) begin to perish.

God-dreams come from knowing Him and connecting with Him regularly and intimately. *God-sized* dreams come from knowing what He can do. To get that God-dream we must take the time to train ourselves upfront. Individuals who are built different don't tell God what their dream is; they ask God what His dream is for them.

WHEN *YOUR* DREAM IS CRUSHED

It can be difficult to give up on your own dream so that God can give you a better one. One time I thought I had my dreams set and my life right on track. The plan was in place and I was raring to go . . . but things didn't go as expected. I experienced a great amount of pain and brokenness in my life, and I felt crushed, rejected, and devastated. It's funny how when things don't go our way, we immediately view ourselves as failures. We tend to associate the presence of pain and struggle with the absence of God, but nothing could be further from the truth.

One day during that period I had a moment that I will never forget. I slipped outside, went out to one of my special places in the woods, and just cried out to God. I was on my knees in 95 degree weather crying, "God can you show up in this place? I need You! I need answers!" Then, out of nowhere, the wind started howling, leaves started flooding down into a pile right in front of me, and the presence of God came over me like I've never felt before. This was no manufactured emotion. God showed up. One moment I was drowning in utter despair, and the next I was basking in absolute peace. His peace that surpassed all understanding flooded me, as wave after wave of His grace washed over me. Within fifteen minutes the Holy Spirit had given me the answer I was looking for.

That was a defining moment for me. As I began walking back, I could see God's bigger picture. I thought, *God has a greater plan for my life . . . a greater purpose. He has given me His dream which is much better than anything I could have ever imagined.*

As sons and daughters of God, our own plans are varied and fickle like the wind, but God's plans are a straight and narrow path that we can follow. I had stalled in pursuing my dreams until I completely let go of them and said, "I don't want them to be mine, but to be Yours. Let Your dreams and passions flourish out of me." Then things began to happen again.

When dreams or plans get crushed, it's an awful feeling. We naturally think, *Well, that's what I had planned for my life and now I have nothing. Now what?* But that's exactly when God can use our moments of powerlessness to draw us closer to and reveal the character of His heart. My friend Max Davis, co-author of this book, wrote a book titled *Desperate Dependence: When You Reach the End, God's Best Begins.* That title says it all, doesn't it?

Take my word for it, hope is never lost. Sometimes it just needs to be redirected and refocused on Christ. God may allow us to come to a point where our dream dies so that His dream can be resurrected. When Jesus hung on the cross and died, everything appeared lost . . . but God wasn't finished. The Bible is filled with such moments.

God specializes in the salvation of the living and the resurrection of the dead. God can restore wasted years and replenish what we have lost, be it from locust invasions (Joel 2:25-32) or other reasons. When you return to Him, He resets and renews you. Nature itself is designed to cycle through death and resurrection. Within the shell of a seed is the promise of what it will become, what it was created to be—an oak, an herb, a flower, or a pumpkin. But until that seed is buried in the ground and dies, it can't be resurrected into its new and intended form. To become our best selves, sometimes our dreams have to die.

Yet when our dreams are crushed and we are uncertain of what to do or where to go, God draws us closer and says, "In the absence of clarity, you have an invitation to intimacy with Me. I will speak into your life through the whisper of the Holy Spirit, and I will tell you where to go."

I love Isaiah 30:21: "Whether you turn to the right or to the left, your ears will hear a voice behind you, saying, 'This is the way; walk in it.'" The New Testament puts it this way, "Since we live by the Spirit, let us keep in step with the Spirit" (Galatians 5:25). Living in the Spirit means being saved. So this passage indicates that it's possible to be saved yet not walk in the Spirit or be led by the Spirit. I want my life to be Spirit led. Those who are built different do too.

PRUNING IS NOT PUNISHMENT

A few years ago, Margaret Feinberg set out to provide a culinary exploration of Scripture through a book she titled *Taste and See: Discovering God among Butchers, Bakers, & Fresh Food Markets*. Recently, I had the opportunity of interviewing her about that book and hearing her reflect on some of her incredible experiences, adventures, and lessons. One of the topics we discussed involved the significance of the grape. Did you know that there are nearly 500 mentions of grapes, vines, wines, or vineyards throughout Scripture? Clearly, God mentioned this fruit and the process through which it is grown, harvested, and prepared for a reason.

To better understand the significance of grapes, Margaret decided to spend extensive time studying, observing, and working alongside a small vintner in Napa Valley, California. One of the most important things she quickly came to understand was the intricacy and detailed attention of the pruning process. Initially, like many of us, she thought pruning was a messy and aimless task involving some type of sharp machete that could possibly cause harm to the grapes and the vines. However, she saw that vines were pruned with little tiny shears. Most vintners would walk through their vineyards many times until they had handled every cluster of grapes, and they would do this three to five times during a growing season. Each time the vintner handled the cluster, he or she would cut off just a leaf or a branch so that every grape on that cluster would receive the maximum amount of air and sunlight in order to produce maximum fruitfulness, growth, and flavor.

With that in mind, look at what Jesus says about the pruning process within our own lives:

> "I am the true vine, and my Father is the gardener. He cuts off every branch in me that bears no fruit, while every branch that does bear fruit he prunes so that it will be even more fruitful. You are already clean because of the word I have spoken to you. Remain in me, as I also remain in you. No branch can bear fruit by itself; it must remain in the vine. Neither can you bear fruit unless you remain in me."
> (John 15:1-4)

In our interview, Margaret went on to share:

> I personally believe most of our understanding of God's pruning in our lives is unhealthy and distorted. When God comes and prunes us, He does it so intimately. His hands are on us, His face is close to us, and He cares so deeply about cutting back or removing the things in our lives which may prohibit us from growing in our maximum fruitfulness and flavor as we bring the flavor of heaven down here to this earth. If that is what God means by pruning, then my prayer is that He would have His way with me.

As I was writing this chapter, Tim Tebow was cut from the Jacksonville Jaguars. He had previously retired from the NFL for eight years, but tried returning as a tight end even though he had a dream of ultimately being a Hall of Fame NFL quarterback. Tebow is one of the hardest workers in the history of the game and had a lot of initial success, winning a National Championship at Florida and the Heisman Trophy. He was on his way. Yet even though he saw some early success leading the Denver Broncos to the AFC Championship game, his NFL career ended early because his coaches didn't utilize his gifts as they might have.

Tebow's disappointing experience has opened other opportunities where he's experiencing great success in broadcasting, spreading the gospel, promoting charities, and just being a positive voice in a negative world. He wasn't afraid to give pro baseball a shot, either. He has remained faithful, he's prepared, and he knows where his identity is. Even when the dreams of a Hall of Fame acknowledgment were pruned from his life, Tim Tebow remained on mission by staying connected to the ultimate Source. He says, "One day we'll see the big picture. One day we'll see how this puzzle's put together, how it all works out. But until then, let's rejoice. Let's remember the Lord is near. And let's express confidence in our God because we trust His plan."[30]

When Tim Tebow hung up his cleats, he was a child of God first and foremost, with the Holy Spirit directing his path and purpose every step of the way. A lot of people "hang up their cleats" at different times in their lives and in different ways. I hung up my baseball cleats after my senior year at Liberty after an honest conversation with a good friend who happens to be a Tampa Bay Rays scout. Sure, I would like to have played pro ball for a couple years, but I felt God tugging on my heart for another purpose . . . and here I am.

When things don't go the way you hope, expect, or even dream of, my prayer is that you realize God isn't punishing you. He may just be pruning and preparing you for something greater!

TEN

WILDERNESS TRAINING

"In God's wilderness lies the hope of the world—the
great fresh unblighted, unredeemed wilderness."

— John Muir

The more I've been thinking about prime examples of people with an "even if . . ." mentality and those who are built different, I keep coming back to the story of David. Back in Chapter 3 we looked at him as a rare model of someone who had an undivided heart. At this point, I want to focus on David again, but from a different perspective. Specifically, I'm intrigued by what enabled David to step up to the plate and face Goliath when not one of the other Israelite warriors moved a muscle.

The Philistines were proposing *representative combat*, a military approach that was familiar in ancient Eastern warfare. One warrior would be chosen by each side, and those two representatives would compete in a one-on-one battle. The army of the loser would be subservient to the other, or at least they were supposed to be. The intent of this arrangement was to minimize bloodshed compared to an all-out war.

However, when the Philistine representative turned out to be approximately nine and a half feet tall, and armed to the hilt, the Israelites no doubt wanted to reconsider the representative combat arrangement. However, they didn't have any better alternatives. From all appearances, they were completely outmatched by the Philistines. Goliath had come out twice a day for forty days, urging the Israelites to send him a competitor, but still no takers.

David was only on the scene because he was delivering grain and bread to his brothers, and a gift of cheese for their commander. But when he happened to hear Goliath's challenge, he couldn't understand why no one else was responding. His inquiries immediately drew the wrath and trash talk of his oldest brother, but he got the attention of King Saul. And frankly, Saul was out of options. *He* certainly didn't want to step out on the field with Goliath, and he couldn't find anyone else who would, either. Despite Saul's doubts and concerns, he eventually relented and decided to let David give it a try. And the rest, as they say, is history.

When given the opportunity, David confidently hurled his slingshot and the stone nailed the giant between the eyes, causing Goliath to hit the ground with a thud like a giant cedar of Lebanon. After the dust settled, instead of submitting (as was the agreement), the Philistine army took off in a panic and the reinvigorated Israelites chased them down.

It all happened because David *fought* differently, and he fought differently because he was *built* different. When people are built different, they find the courage to act when opportunities arise, and they create change that inspires others to engage.

David had been on a simple assignment. As the youngest sibling, he was on the bottom of the pecking order. He was the one who tended sheep while his older brothers served in the army. His task that day was not unlike a middle schooler being told to ride his bike down to the high school and take a sack lunch to his

Senior quarterback brother. The day had begun as another unexciting, uneventful agenda for him. So how did he wind up facing down Goliath when nobody else would?

Part of the answer you should recall from Chapter 8. The reason David rose above the other Israelites—why he was set apart (separated) from them—was because of his preparation. Even though he was low man on the totem pole in his home, he had used all available opportunities to develop new skills and to grow his faith and courage. We get a clue in the argument he gave Saul when trying to get the king's okay to fight Goliath:

> **"Your servant has been keeping his father's sheep. When a lion or a bear came and carried off a sheep from the flock, I went after it, struck it and rescued the sheep from its mouth. When it turned on me, I seized it by its hair, struck it and killed it. . . . The Lord who rescued me from the paw of the lion and the paw of the bear will rescue me from the hand of this Philistine."**
> **(1 Samuel 17:34-37)**

Even before David's showdown with Goliath, he'd had experience in protecting his sheep from danger. For most people, bear wrestling and lion taming would be challenge enough for one lifetime, but with those experiences already on his résumé, David saw the giant as just another critter threatening his flock that needed to be disposed of.

Another reason that David could stand up to Goliath when no one else would is that David's answer to "Why" was directly linked to his "Who." More than just having a vague dream in mind, David knew his purpose—God's purpose for him.

The same is true for us. Only after knowing God (our *Who*) intimately does God reveal our *why*—our gifts and calling. All our gifts and everything we are starts with an intimate relationship with Him. Much of David's preparation in the wilderness was getting to better understand God, his Creator. Even then, it requires time with Him to comprehend our *why*. There are no shortcuts to take. We must want more *of* God before we get more *from* God. Completing this process is critical, and it's where many people run off the rails, even in ministry. Is it God we are in love with, or is it our ministry, or our dreams? Is it God we most desire, or is the relationship based on what He can give us? Only by spending time in the wilderness do we begin to discover and understand the plans and purposes of God for us.

David was prepared for his moment with Goliath because he had an intimate knowledge of who God was. That empowered him. He knew firsthand his God delighted in impossibility. Because David had already killed the bear and the lion in the wilderness, and had honed his skill with the sling God had placed in his hand, he knew that God would do it again. So as he faced Goliath, he didn't have to warm up. He came to play. He was ready.

"God is preparing His heroes," wrote the great theologian and evangelist A.B. Simpson, "and when the opportunity comes He can fit them into their place in a moment and the world will wonder where they came from."[31]

POWER IS FOUND THROUGH SURRENDER

Yes, David had a rare confidence and knowledge of his purpose and his capabilities. After all, it was God who built and breathed it into him and developed it. Yet he had something that set him apart even more. A person can be successful as the world defines it and still not be impactful. It's not just raw talent that matters; it's talent plus something else. The Bible says, "Samuel [the prophet/priest] took the horn of oil and anointed [David] in the presence of his brothers, and from that day on the Spirit of the Lord came powerfully upon David" (1 Samuel 16:13).

Did you notice what else made the difference in David's life? David was built different because he carried the Spirit of the Lord—a rare occurrence in the Old Testament—which gave him a supernatural edge. His confidence in God was so strong that he ran into the battle and was victorious, yet he was also humble, wise, and discerning. The Holy Spirit was his secret sauce, his "it factor."

If you are a believer, you can access the same power that filled David. Prior to Jesus' arrival on earth, select people in specific circumstances felt the power and guidance of the Holy Spirit, but He didn't permanently indwell anyone until after Jesus rose from the dead.

Before Jesus ascended, He explained what would happen: "Very truly I tell you, it is for your good that I am going away. Unless I go away, the Advocate [the Holy Spirit] will not come to you; but if I go, I will send him to you" (John 16:7). Let that sink into your heart and take root. When Jesus could no longer be with His people in person, He promised to send the Holy Spirit "for our good." Paul explained that when we trust Jesus and believe in Him, we are sealed with the Holy Spirit as a guarantee (Ephesians 1:13). That means the Holy Spirit comes to dwell within us. Paul also wrote, "Do you not know that your bodies are temples of the Holy Spirit, who is in you, whom you have received from God?" (1 Corinthians 6:19)

Believers have access to God through the Holy Spirit, but not everyone understands or takes advantage of that benefit. As we saw in the previous chapter, it is possible to live in the Spirit and not walk in the Spirit (Galatians 5:25). Living in the Spirit means to have the Holy Spirit within us. To walk in the Spirit means to keep in step with Him, to yield to His control, follow His lead, and allow Him to exert His influence over us. It is possible for believers to just go through the motions of life without engaging the Holy Spirit. Sadly, many do.

Let me expand the previous passage from 1 Corinthians just a little: "Do you not know that your bodies are temples of the Holy Spirit, who is in you, whom you have received from God? You are not your own; you were bought at a price. Therefore honor God with your bodies" (1 Corinthians 6:19-20). Notice how it is impossible to detach physical actions from spiritual beliefs and commitments, although some philosophies attempt to do so. But you can't willingly sin and maintain a "clean" spirit within.

So how do we honor God with our bodies? It's quite simple. We allow the Holy Spirit within us to have free rein over our lives. Paul says it concisely: "Walk by the Spirit, and you will not gratify the desires of the flesh" (Galatians 5:16).

If *young* believers desire a life of purpose and allow the Holy Spirit to anoint and guide their steps early on, God can set them on the best path for their lives that will maximize their gifts. But all is not lost for *older* believers who got a late start in their relationship with Christ. God is a master of using our past blunders to teach us, and of redeeming our time for maximum impact. The point is, whatever age you are, *now* is the time to embrace the Holy Spirit of God and let Him start empowering your life. When we implement the habit of surrender, we will learn the power of His strength.

LESSONS FROM THE WILDERNESS

Interestingly, even after David had been anointed king and the Holy Spirit was on him, he continued in the wilderness, tending the sheep. Even after his impressive victory over Goliath, he didn't run up to Saul and say, "Move over! There's a new king in town." In fact, David was determined to let God decide on the right time for the transfer of power, and he spent many long stressful months on the run from King's Saul's jealous rage and death threats.

And while David was in the wilderness, whether tending sheep or on the run, he was developing character and maturity. It was there, alone on the hillsides, that he got to know God intimately. He became skillful at swinging a sling, and also at playing stringed instruments for praise and worship. David loved to worship God. Praise and worship would be at the foundation of his reign as king and his writing of the Psalms. His musical gifts were even used to soothe Saul's anxiety as David played his lyre for the king (1 Samuel 16:23). For David, the wilderness was a time of preparation, and he used much of what he learned there throughout his lifetime to make him a better king and stronger follower of God.

David's best-known psalm reflects the depth of his relationship with God:

The Lord is my shepherd, I lack nothing.
He makes me lie down in green pastures,
he leads me beside quiet waters,
he refreshes my soul.
He guides me along the right paths for his name's sake.
Even though I walk through the darkest valley, I will fear no
evil, for you are with me;
your rod and your staff, they comfort me.
You prepare a table before me in the presence of
my enemies.
You anoint my head with oil; my cup overflows.
Surely your goodness and love will follow me all the days of
my life,
and I will dwell in the house of the Lord forever.
(Psalm 23)

Those who are built different learn to walk in the Spirit. Anchored in the Bible, they let the Holy Spirit guide and develop them into the individuals God desires them to be. They are like David, warriors who make a difference in their own generations—among their families and circles of influence. They carry the anointing and presence of God into every battlefield and area of ministry. Your age or station in life doesn't matter. God wants to use you right where you are.

I realize that not many people get the same opportunities I've had at my age. As a young man starting out in life and ministry, I've been part of an incredible organization. I've had the privilege of meeting, interviewing, and learning from some of the most committed spiritual men and women of God in our world today. They have influenced me heavily and are living examples of being built different.

I recently did a *Built Different* podcast with *New York Times* best-selling author Mo Isom Aiken. She said that "every person is extended an invitation to be filled with the Spirit of God, to no longer be bound by the strongholds in their life, to walk with Him, and to experience the full inheritance we have in Christ."

That's what I want. I want to be built different. I want to make choices that set me apart and to be defined by the Spirit of God in my life. And that's what I want for you too, regardless of age, gender, or ethnicity. Our culture is screaming for us to stand up to our Goliaths and step up into our moments.

We all have wilderness periods of life where circumstances aren't as pleasant or as comfortable as we might like. When you find yourself in one, don't assume you're alone. Others have been through very similar periods. And don't assume you've done something wrong, because God may be preparing you for something better. This separation may indeed be preparation. After all,

Moses, David, John the Baptist, Paul, and even Jesus spent time in the wilderness before they were launched into their destiny.

Don't waste the time you are given in the wilderness. God is there with you, and there's no better opportunity to get to know Him better. We'll look at this concept a bit closer in the next chapter.

ELEVEN

ADVANCED WILDERNESS TRAINING

"The wilderness holds answers to questions man has not yet learned how to ask."

— Nancy Newhall, Conservationist

On January 8, 2018, the #1 Alabama Crimson Tide were set to face off against the #3 team in the country, the Georgia Bulldogs. This College Football Playoff national championship game had been highly anticipated as both were SEC powerhouses with similar records—Alabama was 12-1 while Georgia was 13-1. Alabama had a lot on the line because a victory would secure coach Nick Saban's place in history by tying the great Bear Bryant with a sixth National Championship. It looked good for them, too. Many of the players on their roster that year would go on to be NFL first-round draft picks.

However, the first half of this National Championship game belonged to the Bulldogs. It seemed as if things couldn't have gone worse for the Crimson Tide as their offense behind quarterback Jalen Hurts couldn't get anything going. Sloppy and undisciplined play, accompanied by a lack of execution, led to only 89 first-half yards, with a mere 21 of them through the air. At halftime, the seemingly deflated Alabama team trailed 13-0.

Everyone wondered what Nick Saban would do to turn things around, but no one could have guessed his next move. He benched Jalen Hurts, his sophomore phenom with a 26-2 record who was First-Team All SEC and reigning SEC Offensive Player of the Year. Who could possibly replace Hurts? Saban put in Tua Tagovailoa, a true Freshman who'd had very minimal game experience.

Tagovailoa made some rookie mistakes, but performed exceptionally, overall. Alabama never gave up, and by the end of the fourth quarter had tied Georgia, 20-20. And with mere seconds on the clock, Alabama only needed to punch in a 36-yard field goal for the win, but they missed it. The game went into overtime.

Georgia scored first in overtime with a 51-yard field goal. On Alabama's first play, Tagovailoa was sacked and lost sixteen yards. But on the very next play, he connected on a 41-yard touchdown pass . . . to another freshman . . . to win the national championship game. Final score: Georgia 23, Alabama 26.

Ironically, the previous season Alabama had lost the College Football Playoff national championship much like Georgia did in 2018. Coach Saban hadn't forgotten it. He said in a post-game interview: "I could not believe it. There's lots of highs and lows. Last year we lost on the last play of the game and this year we won on the last play of the game. These kids really responded the right way. We said last year, 'Don't waste the feeling.' They sure didn't, the way they played tonight."[32]

"Don't waste the feeling." Great advice! Hang on to that lousy feeling, that lie others tell us (or we tell ourselves) that we just aren't good enough. Then, when the opportunity comes for us to prove them (or ourselves) wrong, the satisfaction of success feels that much better. Don't waste the feeling. Don't waste what you're learning as you wait until you can achieve your desired goals. Don't waste your time in the wilderness. Those periods are not wastes of time; they are investments into your character, perseverance, and inner strength.

PATIENT DOESN'T MEAN STAGNANT

People too often equate waiting seasons as stagnant seasons. They wind up going through the motions, wishing things were different, and complaining when they're not. However, waiting seasons should never be an excuse for a lack of motivation; they should be viewed through the lens of hopeful expectation. You can view your wilderness as an opportunity rather than an obstacle.

Gandhi once said, "To lose patience is to lose the battle." Loss of patience leads to panic, and panic can cause us to make mistakes. When waiting, we begin to grow anxious, discouraged, or disappointed. Instead of holding out for the best time and place to act, we take matters into our own hands and try to hustle things along. We forget that our timing is not always God's timing. Besides, if we keep our focus on the future, we tend to neglect the significance of today.

But what happens when we don't get the results or the raise or the response we want? What happens when we're out there pouring our souls into our projects and working our fingers to the bone, but feel like we're not getting anything in return? Then what? Musician Hoyt Axton wrote, "Work your fingers to the bone, and what do you get? Bony fingers!" But worse than that, becoming too performance-based or results-driven takes our eyes off the importance of what we're doing and focuses our attention on a scoreboard or stat sheet. If we aren't anchored and centered in something greater than merely finishing the next project, tough times will leave us reaching for anything to numb or anesthetize our pain during the wait.

Jon Gordon writes, "No matter what anyone says, just show up and do the work. If they praise you, show up and do the work. If they criticize you, show up and do the work. If no one even notices you, just show up and do the work."[33]

Sometimes we just have to keep on keeping on, knowing and believing that God is much more interested in how He's making us than in where He's taking us. In other words, God often does things *in* us before He will do things *for* us. I love the words of Galatians 6:9 which remind us, "Let us not become weary in doing good, for at the proper time we will reap a harvest if we do not give up."

MAKING THE MOST OF YOUR WILDERNESS

In the previous chapter we considered how David trained as a shepherd in the hills of the Judean wilderness and protected his flock from lions and bears. But here's another question: Have you ever wondered what made David risk his life to rescue a sheep from the mouth of a lion or a bear? When trying to convince Saul that he was up to the task of facing Goliath, David told him, *"Your servant has been keeping his father's sheep. When a lion or a bear came and carried off a sheep from the flock, I went after it, struck it and rescued the sheep from its mouth. When it turned on me, I seized it by its hair, struck it and killed it"* (1 Samuel 17:34-35). That should give us some insight into David's psyche and physical stature. We know he was a handsome young man, but here we see he was also a mighty warrior, preparing for his moment. It seems he wrestled those wild beasts like a WWE superstar.

It's one thing to risk life and limb in a battle where fame and fortune are the ultimate rewards. But why would David risk his life for a single sheep when he could instead walk away and consider it a reasonable loss? A few reasons pop out to me that may help us wrestle our own lions and bears.

First, David clearly loved his sheep. Envision the scene. As the flock grazes, David's probably sitting under a tree, maybe strumming on his lyre. He's familiar with each member of the group—age, wounds, illnesses, eating habits, etc. David knew his sheep, so he becomes concerned when he hears a distressed sound, almost like a baby's cry, different from all the other bleats. His ears perk up. A lion has isolated one of the group and is preparing to pounce. David responds instinctively. He rushes toward the sound, and before the lion can close in on its prey, he wrestles the predator to the ground. An average shepherd would just let the lion take one of the flock and go on its way. Not David. Every one of his sheep were important.

Second, tending sheep was David's primary responsibility at that time. It was where God had placed him. Too often we dwell so much on the past or the future that we forget to embrace the gift of the present. I don't think David's biggest dream was to be a shepherd his entire lifetime, yet he was still committed to doing his best where God had him planted. He wasn't grumbling or complaining. He worshiped, was faithful, and protected His sheep. He was willing to risk his life to defend a single sheep from the lions and bears because he cared that much about what he was doing. He knew he was a son, not just of Jesse, but of God, worshiping and working for the ultimate King.

Third, God met David in the wilderness. As we saw earlier, it's where he got to know his *Who*. God helped him tend those sheep in the wilderness. David told King Saul, *"The Lord . . . rescued me from the paw of the lion and the paw of the bear"* (1 Samuel 17:37). God didn't just show up in David's life when he stood before Goliath; He showed up long before that, in the wilderness.

During wilderness experiences, some people perceive their situation as a sentence to be served. Some of them shut down and figuratively pull the covers of life up over their heads until things get better. Others buckle down, grit their teeth, and determine to get through it, come what may—a better option, to be sure, but they're still seeing this time as a sentence to be served before being pardoned or paroled. The next time you're facing a wilderness experience of your own, try taking a deep breath, looking around, and seeing what you can learn from it. God is nearby; look for Him. If your friends and family aren't too far off, see what you can do for them. Use that time not as a disaster or prison sentence, but as an opportunity for adventure. Don't just endure your wilderness experiences; conquer them. Come out on top.

During such times, God wants to meet you right where you are—deepest valley, driest wilderness, algebra class, at the sink doing dishes, changing diapers (again!) . . . anywhere! Then, the wonder of your relationship is understanding that He loves you so much that He doesn't want you to stay stuck where you are. God wants to walk you through your wilderness, and in His timing and perfect plan, He will then help you maneuver and navigate your way out of it. He loves you, so He appreciates and rewards whatever you are doing for Him.

When God shuts certain doors in our lives, we have a habit of sticking our foot in the doorway to prevent it from totally closing. However, sometimes we need to let that door slam shut and let God do His work while we're standing in the hallway. When the time is right, God will either reopen that same door with you being more prepared, or He'll open another door that you didn't even know was there! Patience is the understanding that God prepares us when we are faithful wherever He has us.

John Maxwell points out:

> Noah—waited 120 years before the predicted rains arrived.
> Abraham—waited 25 years for a promised son.
> Joseph—waited 14 years in prison for a crime he didn't commit.
> Job—waited perhaps a lifetime, 60-70 years, for God's justice.
>
> God prepares leaders in a Crock-Pot, not in a microwave oven. More important than the awaited goal is the work God does in us while we wait."[34]

The truth is, God may not change our circumstances this side of heaven. Things may not get easier. But when we invite Him into the midst of our waiting seasons in life, He often refines, restores, and rebuilds us, strengthening us to endure those long, challenging, mundane circumstances. The Apostle Paul challenged the Thessalonian church to "Rejoice always, pray continually, give thanks in all circumstances; for this is God's will for you in Christ Jesus" (1 Thessalonians 5:16-18).

Here's the question: Why don't you let the one who was always meant to be in control, be in control of your life? What do you have to lose? It may be scary and uncertain, but when we place our trust in Him, He instills within us a newfound confidence and hopeful expectation for the future. As Brandon Lake recently said while leading worship at one of our events, "Expectancy is the breeding ground for miracles."

My prayer is that you would be confident in knowing that we serve a God who delights in impossibility! Trust Him! Your breakthrough may be just around the corner.

TWELVE

PITFALLS AND SECOND CHANCES

"The lowest ebb is the turn of the tide."

—Henry Wadsworth Longfellow

A minister friend of mine once had a flight delayed overnight. It's a fairly common occurrence for people who travel a lot, but in this case he was very upset because he had an important schedule to meet. Additionally, because of circumstances beyond his control, he had to spend the night in the terminal, which is never fun. At 3 a.m., frustrated and unable to sleep, he bumped into another man whose flight had also been delayed, and they struck up a conversation. As they talked, the stranger began to pour his heart out to my minister friend. To make a long story short, the stranger was craving the living water of Jesus and my friend was an obedient vessel carrying a fresh supply! The other man came to Jesus and his life was radically changed. He and my friend are still very close to this day—all because of an uncomfortable disruption that God turned into a holy event.

Every story has more than one potential ending, depending on how the characters in it respond. If my minister friend had taken out his frustration on the next stranger he met, his story would be not nearly as inspiring. But because he was responsive to the Holy Spirit in the wee hours of a disheartening day, a new child of God was added to the kingdom.

LIVING IN SOMEONE ELSE'S SHADOW

I want to consider another potential ending to one of the stories I told in the previous chapter. In describing the heroics of Tua Tagovailoa coming off the bench and completely turning around a championship game for Alabama, I would be remiss not to mention Jalen Hurts's perspective as the quarterback who was yanked from the game at halftime.

As we saw, Tua Tagovailoa was a player who had prepared and was ready to seize the opportunity when his moment came. That's a powerful testimony. However, think how difficult Nick Saban's change of quarterbacks would have been for the guy who had been the staple of the program during his first two seasons, leading Alabama to a 26-2 record and being dubbed perhaps the best quarterback in college football at the time. Up to that point, Jalen Hurts had done everything with class. He had performed under pressure. He had led multiple come-from-behind victories throughout his career. But with this sudden change at halftime of the 2018 CFP National Championship Game, Hurts had a decision to make. Would he allow this demotion to make him bitter? Would this be the disruption that crushed his spirit and caused him to settle for an unfulfilling final destination?

After the Crimson Tide seemed to have found their new star and potential team leader in Tua Tagovailoa, Jalen Hurts could have allowed that to impact his confidence and self-worth. Moments like those have ruined many athletes' careers, but Jalen Hurts is built different. As Alabama rolled into the offseason, everyone was asking if Hurts would stay at Alabama and have to compete for the starting job next season, or transfer out and start somewhere fresh? It was with great courage, discernment, strength, and humility that Hurts decided to return to Alabama for his junior season. He would wind up being named the backup behind Tua for most of the 2018 campaign.

And because of that decision, it was during the 2018 SEC Championship game, after Tua got injured, that the world got to see what Jalen Hurts was truly made of. That day Hurts led the Alabama Crimson Tide to a come-from-behind victory over the very same team that got him benched the previous year, the Georgia Bulldogs. His painful disruption had not made him bitter. He had allowed it to make him *better*. I believe one of the greatest lessons we can learn from this story is that God is more concerned with our *character* than He is our *comfort*. Sometimes God may allow disruptions in your life so you can get realigned and become better equipped for the destiny He has prepared for you.

Following that SEC Championship game, Nick Saban was asked about the gutsy performance of Jalen Hurts. He replied, "I've probably never been prouder of a player than Jalen. It's unprecedented to have a guy that won as many games as he won . . . start as a freshman, only lose a couple of games the whole time he was the starter, and then all of a sudden, he's not the quarterback anymore. How do you manage that? How do you handle that? You've got to have a tremendous amount of class and character to put team first, knowing your situation is not what it used to be."[35] A couple of weeks after the victory, Coach Saban was still praising him: "Jalen was an example for people all over the country in terms of a guy persevering. He won the 'most inspirational player' on his team voted on by teammates. He didn't win that when he was going 26-2 as a starter, he won it when he was the backup and working every day to affect people in a positive way."[36]

Jalen Hurts realized that what disrupted him didn't have to define or defeat him. He kept showing up. He kept working hard. He allowed adversity to sharpen not only his skills as a football player, but also his character, humility, leadership, and team-first commitment. With this never-quit mindset of perseverance, Jalen realized that a situation that threatened his purpose could also reveal the potential and promise God had destined for his life.

After leading the Crimson Tide to that 2018 SEC title, the following year Jalen transferred to the University of Oklahoma where he not only received the starting position, but eventually became runner-up for the 2019 Heisman trophy and was recognized as one of college football's top players. And as the Lord has scripted the rest of this amazing story, Jalen went on to be chosen by the Philadelphia Eagles in the second round of the 2020 NFL Draft, and he remains their starting quarterback after leading the Eagles to the 2022 Super Bowl. He recently signed as the highest-paid player in NFL history—not bad for a guy who was benched and remanded to backup with his career in jeopardy during his junior season of college football. He's now shining under the brightest lights of the biggest arenas. Why? Because he never gave up.

PITFALLS VS. PIT STOPS

For those who have an "even if . . ." mindset, disruptions often become their most powerful areas of ministry. When they see God working, even if the worst has happened to them, then impending destruction becomes a holy disruption. Their test becomes a testimony.

Consider the Apostle Paul. After preaching the gospel all over the Mediterranean, he felt a distinct direction from God to testify before Caesar in Rome. He had wanted to go to Rome, but he didn't reach his destination without several major disruptions:

> It started when he returned from one of his journeys and went through a purification rite with other Jewish men, but was then falsely accused of taking Gentiles into the temple (Acts 21:17-29).

> Many took offense at this false news, dragged Paul from the temple, tried to kill him, and created an uproar throughout the whole city (Acts 21:30-31).

> The Roman commander arrived to restore peace, but mistook Paul for an Egyptian terrorist and had him arrested and bound with chains (Acts 21:32-39).

> Paul was allowed to address the crowd, but when they heard his story they again became hostile (Acts 21:40—22:22).

> The Roman commander moved Paul into the barracks and ordered that he be flogged, but retracted the order as soon as he discovered Paul was a Roman citizen (Acts 22:23-29).

> Wanting to know exactly what Paul had done wrong, the Roman commander assembled the Jewish Sanhedrin, where Paul got punched in the mouth before a violent dispute arose that threatened to tear him to pieces (Acts 23:30—23:11).

> While Paul was in protective custody, a plot was hatched to kill him, but he found out about it and the Romans transferred him to Caesarea for his own protection (Acts 23:12-35).

> Paul's accusers traveled to Caesarea to try him before the governor, Felix, who heard the case but would make no final ruling. He was holding out for a bribe, and kept Paul in prison (though with considerable freedom) for two years until a new governor was appointed (Acts 24).

> The new governor, Festus, got to Paul's trial quickly. But when he suggested having Paul returned to Jerusalem, Paul knew he would be in danger there, and immediately appealed to Caesar which was his right as a Roman citizen.

That series of disruptions in Paul's life was how he found himself under Roman guard and on a ship with a couple hundred other prisoners, a centurion, a band of soldiers, and the crew. But he was finally sailing toward his dream of going to Rome. Yes, Paul was a prisoner, but he was on his way to completing his divine assignment. Have you ever considered the possibility that what has you in chains could be God's vehicle to get you where He wants you to be?

You'd think by now Paul would have had enough disruptions to last him a lifetime, that he deserved a long period of smooth sailing. But no. His situation got even worse. The ship got caught smack-dab in the middle of a furious hurricane.

Before the storm, Paul sensed in his spirit that something wasn't right, and he tried to convince his centurion overseer, but the Roman listened to the pilot and ship's owner instead. When the violent Northeaster hit, the ship was badly battered. The crew threw the cargo and tackle overboard to keep from sinking, yet the storm just kept pounding them for days until they gave up all hope of being saved. That's what disruptions do. They tempt us to give up hope and abandon our assignment. But Paul was built different.

He had the guidance of the Holy Spirit which gave him God's favor and extended that favor to everyone aboard.

That night, while the ship was getting slammed and everybody on board except Paul was fearing for their lives, an angel appeared at Paul's bedside and told him not to be afraid, that he *must* appear before Caesar, and that by God's grace none on board would lose their lives. When God calls you to an assignment, all hell may break loose against you, but it will never stop His will from being accomplished . . . and He will see you through it.

Since Paul was the only calm person on board, he became the mouthpiece for God and sound wisdom. Suddenly, everyone was listening to him—the soldiers, the officers, the crew, and the other prisoners. He told them what God had said and urged them to take courage. He also gave them some practical things to do, which they readily responded to. The fact that Paul was a prisoner no longer mattered; everyone aboard knew he was a man of God with the Holy Spirit in him. That's what happens to those who are built different: when going through storms, they become anchors and examples for those around them (Acts 27).

The ship eventually crashed ashore on the Island of Malta. Islanders noted the sailors' plight and came out to greet them with refreshing kindness. It was raining and cold while setting up camp on the beach. Paul was doing his part, gathering a bundle of firewood. The heat revived a dormant viper that bit into Paul's hand and dangled there until he shook it off into the fire. Onlookers expected him to drop dead any second, but nothing happened, which made the natives think he must be a god. For the crew and prisoners, it was more evidence that something holy was at work in Paul's life.

The governor of the island lived in a big plantation nearby. The islanders knew that his father was sick to the point of death, so they rushed Paul to see him. Paul prayed, the man was healed, and news spread like wildfire. Everybody on the island who was sick was brought to Paul. He preached the gospel and prayed for them, and they were healed.

The survivors were on Malta for three months while they arranged for another ship and restocked on supplies. Being arrested and held with the other prisoners, and then undergoing the violent storm were just two more disruptions for Paul. Yet because he saw purpose in his pain, God used him and turned the situation into a *holy* disruption. And Paul finally made it to Rome and built up the young church there as he preached from his own rented house for two whole years "with all boldness and without hindrance" (Acts 28:30).

I think Paul's lesson is, "Don't wait for perfect circumstances to be used of God, because they will never be perfect. God wants to use you right now, where you are at, dealing with whatever uncomfortable situation you are in." I once heard a pastor say, "People come to me all the time telling me they feel called to the mission field. I ask them, 'Have you gone across the street? God's not going to send you overseas if you aren't faithful where you already are.'"

Even if just one soul is touched, it's worth the effort. Sometimes God allows things to disrupt our path to redirect us by placing us in a position to reach one soul. And remember, disruptions need not stop you from reaching your God-given goal.

In fact, God can even use full-fledged tragedies for His purposes. My best friend and his family were on their way home from church one Sunday night when they were hit head-on by a man who was drinking and driving. The accident was so horrific that medical doctors doubted any of them would live. Yet all four survived, although they are still battling and overcoming significant injuries seventeen years later. Thousands of stitches and staples, dozens of injured muscles and broken bones, and even a traumatic brain injury haven't distracted this family away from God's power and sovereignty in all their pain.

We serve a God who can take tragedy and turn it into triumph! What appeared to be an ending, became a new beginning. God has since called the family to start a ministry of their own called Hope Out Loud, where God uses them to reach and impact more lives than they could probably have ever imagined before the wreck.

Whether your disruption is getting benched, being ship-wrecked, having a delayed flight, surviving a near-life-ending car accident, or anything else, God's Spirit wants to turn it into a holy disruption and a powerful testimony of His grace.

Times will come where we must endure the hardship to fully appreciate the healing. Second Corinthians 4:17 says, "For our light and momentary troubles are achieving for us an eternal glory that far outweighs them all." My prayer for you is that you would realize that God sees you, hears you, understands you, and loves you beyond measure. I know it may feel difficult right now and I know it may hurt, but God will never waste your wounds. Cling to the promise of Romans 8:28: "We know that in all things God works for the good of those who love him, who have been called according to His purpose." Again, that "good" may not change your external circumstances. Yet when we invite God into the midst of our mess, the real change takes place internally as He transforms our hearts, renews our minds, and reshapes our perspectives. Just because our lives may look and feel like a mess doesn't mean that God has messed up. When we understand that God is in control and is bigger than whatever is threatening us, every disruption may actually become a precious gift.

THIRTEEN

DISRUPTIONS VS. DESTINY

"God has a purpose for your pain, a reason for your
struggles, and a gift for your faithfulness. Don't give up.
You can't beat a person who doesn't quit."

— John Mason

You may know Kirk Cousins as the Minnesota Vikings quarterback who was twice named a First Team Pro Bowl selection and dubbed by ESPN as the "most accurate passer in the league."[37] Off the field, Kirk is known as a good guy, and he recently received official acknowledgement of that fact: the 2023 Korey Stringer Media Good Guy Award. His confidence motivates fans and carries them through the ups and downs of every football season.

How he got there is quite a story, one that Kirk shared with me years ago in a conversation on our "Ignite Men's Battle Cry" Podcast. Kirk played football throughout high school, and like many other young men in America had expectations of playing in college and, hopefully, the NFL. But during his junior year, he broke his ankle. It was the prime recruiting time for colleges, so it was a threatening disruption. Driving back from the hospital with a cast on his ankle and tears in his eyes, he called his dad and said, "I'm going to miss this season. It means that I can't play in college and the dream is over."

"You don't know that, Kirk," his minister dad replied. "Think of Proverbs 3:5-6: 'Trust in the Lord with all your heart and lean not on your understanding, in all your ways submit to him, and he will direct your steps.'"

At that moment, amid this threatening disruption, seventeen-year-old Kirk Cousins made Proverbs 3:5-6 his life verse. He told himself that from that moment on he was going to trust God and let Him sort out the rest. As it turned out, Kirk did get some playing time before college. In fact, he finished high school with 3,204 passing yards, 40 touchdowns, and 18 interceptions . . . but still no offers of a college scholarship. Once again, Kirk's dreams appeared crushed. But at the very last minute, Michigan State saw no one had snagged him and offered Kirk a chance to play. It was the only offer he received, but then, Michigan State just so happened to be his top choice. He says, "A year and a half earlier I thought it would be impossible to play college football, and now I'm signing to play for a school that was my dream school all along."

Kirk was starting to understand what it meant to walk by faith and trust God as his spiritual journey interwove with his football journey. When he began his career at Michigan State, he sensed the Spirit of God prompting him to remain faithful and keep trusting Him. He excelled in college, becoming Michigan State's all-time record holder in pass completions, yards, and touchdowns. Kirk continued to trust God and set his sight on the NFL.

The night before the NFL draft, his family gathered as his dad read from 1 Samuel 16, describing how David had been anointed king. Kirk's dad pointed out that this passage had the feel of a sports draft because the prophet Samuel showed up at David's house and told his father Jesse to bring out his sons because one of them would be the next king. David had seven older brothers, and one by one they came and stood before Samuel. Several looked quite impressive, but each time, God told Samuel it wasn't the one. Jesse hadn't even included David in the lineup because someone had to tend to the sheep. He sent for David, and as soon as David arrived, God told Samuel, "Rise and anoint him; this is the one" (1 Samuel 16:12). God also explained that the others had been rejected because "people look at the outward appearance, but the Lord looks at the heart" (v. 7).

After reading the story, Kirk's dad told him, "Kirk, lots of people are looking at outward appearances right now with the draft, and that will continue. Ultimately, as you've seen through your upbringing, the Lord directs your steps. The Lord has His hand on your life and the Lord is not looking at the outward appearance. The Lord is looking at the heart. Kirk, you have heart."

NFL drafts usually include ten or so quarterbacks each year. The next day Kirk was the 102nd overall player, picked way down in the fourth round by the Washington Redskins. He was drafted to be the backup to a Heisman Trophy winner. Kirk's dad later asked him, "Kirk do you know how many quarterbacks were picked before you?" Kirk said, "No, I don't." Kirk's dad said, "You were the eighth quarterback . . . and David was the eighth son of Jesse. I think the Lord is speaking to you. He's saying, 'Kirk I have My hand on your life, and when you go to Washington just trust that I've got the next year or two or three—or whatever it may be—under My control.'"

Kirk became the starting quarterback in Washington and then signed with the Minnesota Vikings in 2018. Even after all his success, he'd be the first to tell you that God is faithful and worthy, no matter what. It's significant that Kirk's number at Michigan State was number 8 and he wears number 8 to this day.

Kirk shared with me, "When I look back, I see God's faithfulness all those times I was convinced my career was over. Ultimately, I want people to experience something far greater than football. I want to see lives changed for the kingdom and as many people as possible to come to know the hope of the gospel—not only to come to know Jesus through the gospel, but then to make Him Lord of their life. . . . That's what I want my life to be about."[38]

BEYOND THE DISRUPTIONS

A disruption is somewhat like a condensed, intensified wilderness experience. In the wilderness, time crawls. Nothing appears to be happening on schedule, because you have no schedule. You have plenty of time for reflection as you ponder your life. The Israelite wilderness experience was mandated after God had led them all the way to the Promised Land, yet after arriving and discovering that the land was possessed by some rather large inhabitants, the people rebelled and insisted on returning to Egypt. When Moses, Aaron, and others tried to convince them otherwise, the rebels planned to stone them.

So God stepped in. Plan A was for Him to kill all the rebels—essentially the entire nation—and let Moses start from scratch with a "greater and stronger" nation. But Moses interceded for the people and God relented. But the consequence of their great lack of faith would be to wander in the wilderness until all the unfaithful complainers had died off. Other than a dozen spies, none of them would ever set foot in the Promised Land although they had been right at the border (Numbers 13—14). But forty years later a new generation of more determined, more faithful Israelites returned to take possession of the land under Joshua. Their wilderness experience had been transformative.

A disruption, in contrast, is something that interrupts us while we are actively doing what we are called to do. A wilderness develops us slowly; a disruption threatens to stop us immediately! A lion dragging off one of your sheep in the wilderness is a disruption. So often, disruptions make us feel that everything is over, that we're headed for shipwreck. But just as we've seen that the way we handle our wilderness experiences determines our future, we must also learn to address our disruptions and get past them.

Someone who underwent more than his fair share of both wilderness experiences and disruptions was Joseph, the Old Testament son of Jacob (Israel). Joseph was no ordinary Joe. He first shows up as a teenager, his father's favorite of twelve sons, and more than a little spoiled. Still, he had a dream from God and eventually developed an intimate relationship with Him. Joseph knew his *Who* and comprehended his *why*, which kept him on track as he was drawn to his destiny. He was built different and had the "even if . . ." mindset that kept him determined to trust God no matter what.

But Joseph's brothers weren't so enamored with him. After Jacob made him a special coat, Joseph's ten older brothers "hated him" (Genesis 37:4). And it didn't help when he shared his two divine dreams with them that indicated he would become a leader and his family would bow down to him. His brothers' hatred was rooted in jealousy (Genesis 37:5-11).

As his story develops, Joseph experiences disruption after disruption and a wilderness of incarceration for over a decade. The pressure of one trying circumstance after another brought out a diamond in the rough and revealed his true character. His trust in God and awareness of his ultimate purpose sustained Joseph when life began to unravel . . . and stayed unraveled for a very long time.

DISRUPTION #1: THE PIT

While Joseph's older brothers were out tending the family's flocks, Jacob sent Joseph to check up on them and report back. When they saw him coming in the distance, they conspired: "Here comes that dreamer! Come now, let's kill him and throw him into one of these cisterns and say that a ferocious animal devoured him" (Genesis 37:19-20). The oldest brother, Reuben, convinced them instead to avoid bloodshed and simply throw Joseph in the cistern and leave him there (Genesis 37:21-22). They agreed, and then callously sat down to have lunch. Without someone's help, Joseph was destined to die in there. (Reuben's intent was to rescue Joseph later and return him to his father.)

We sometimes find ourselves in the pits of life that are too much for us to handle alone. No matter how strong we believe we are, we can't get out on our own. I can only imagine what Joseph must have been thinking. Thankfully, he wasn't down there too long, because while his brothers were eating they saw a caravan passing in the distance.

As painful as it must have been for Joseph, God's fingerprints were all over this disruption. It was no coincidence that a caravan heading to Egypt "just happened by" at that moment. Reuben had left for a while, but the others came up with a new plan: why let our brother die in a pit when we can make a few bucks off of him? Let's sell him. Then we'll kill a goat, rip Joseph's fancy coat to shreds, smear the goat's blood on it, and tell our father a wild animal ate him. And that's what they did. Their annoying brother was gone, and in his place they had twenty shekels of silver (which must have divided nicely among ten brothers).

Meanwhile, the caravan took Joseph to Egypt where he would be sold as a slave. This demonstrates the beauty, yet complexity, of God's perfect plan for our lives. Sometimes our circumstances don't turn out the way we expect or want them to go, but that doesn't mean we've been abandoned or neglected. Sometimes God is working in mysterious ways by using our hardest and most challenging situations to provide guidance and produce within us character and perseverance. In good times and in bad, He is constantly working on our behalf.

DISRUPTION #2: POTIPHAR'S WIFE

In Egypt, Joseph was sold to a prominent government official named Potiphar. As time passed, God's favor began to shine on Joseph to the point that Potiphar entrusted his entire estate to Joseph to oversee (Genesis 39:1-6). Though no doubt a little homesick for his father, Joseph's situation was looking up and life wasn't so bad.

In addition to his exceptional administrative abilities, Joseph was also "well-built and handsome" (Genesis 39:6). In time, he captured the attention of Potiphar's wife, and he discovered that disruptions can come in the form of temptation. She started coming to him "day after day," and she wasn't subtle about what she wanted: "Come to bed with me!" (Genesis 39:7, 10) It was a tempting opportunity much like the one David had with Bathsheba, and one that millions of people have faced since then: "No one is looking. I wonder what I can 'get away with'?"

But unlike King David with Bathsheba, Joseph held fast to his morals and standards. He tried to reason with Potiphar's wife: "My master has withheld nothing from me except you, because you are his wife. How then could I do such a wicked thing and sin against God?" (Genesis 39:9) In addition to not wanting to offend God or tarnish his reputation, Joseph didn't want to forfeit his divine destiny.

Potiphar's wife must have been stunned and humiliated at Joseph's repeated rejection. I suspect she was under conviction too. Who was this upstart slave to deny her advances . . . and then to take the moral high ground? She must have believed she was every man's fantasy because she kept coming after Joseph until one day she made a mad grab for him. Joseph literally ran from temptation, leaving his cloak clutched in her hands.

DISRUPTION #3: FALSE ACCUSATIONS AND IMPRISONMENT

You'd think Joseph would be rewarded for his integrity, but this was a classic example of the old saying, "Hell hath no fury like a woman scorned." With Joseph's cloak in her possession, Potiphar's wife flipped the script and created an elaborate lie to tell her husband: "Look, this Hebrew has been brought to us to make sport of us! He came in here to sleep with me, but I screamed. When he heard me scream for help, he left his cloak beside me and ran out of the house" (Genesis 39:14-15).

Joseph tried to defend himself, but Potiphar sided with his wife. Potiphar was captain of the guard and threw Joseph into the jail where the king's prisoners were confined. John Wesley wrote in his commentary, "Potiphar, it is likely, chose that prison because it was the worst."[39] It was a dungeon, not the Ritz. Things weren't looking too good for Joseph. He had gone from the pit, to the slave auction block, to incarcerated felon.

Sitting in that dungy prison day after day, month after month, year after year, Joseph must have recalled his teenage dreams and thought, *God, what about my destiny? My life is the complete opposite of what You said it would be.* I'm sure he experienced doubt, discouragement, and discontentment.

Yet he remained faithful to God. Joseph worshiped God through his work in that wilderness/prison and something amazing happened. The Bible says, "The warden put Joseph in charge of all those held in the prison, and he was made responsible for all that was done there. The warden paid no attention to anything under Joseph's care, because the Lord was with Joseph and gave him success in whatever he did" (Genesis 39:22-23). God had enabled Joseph to prosper as a slave under Potiphar, and then as an inmate in a prison. We can prosper in our workplaces or our "prisons" whatever they may be, but we must first be built different.

You may be familiar with the rest of the story. Pharaoh's cupbearer and baker both got tossed into the dungeon because they offended him, where they met Joseph. Both had troubling dreams, which Joseph correctly interpreted. The cupbearer's dream was good news: Pharaoh would reinstate him in three days. The baker's news was not so good: in three days he would be executed (Genesis 40). Joseph asked the cupbearer for a small favor after he was released. He wanted the cupbearer to use his influence with Pharaoh to get Joseph a hearing and possible pardon. But the cupbearer immediately forgot about him. Joseph must have been devastated again, but still, God was in control.

Two more years passed until one night Pharaoh had two disturbing dreams, causing him great distress because none of his magicians or wise men could tell him what they meant. This gave the cupbearer a flash of déjà vu, and he finally remembered Joseph and told Pharaoh all about him. Pharaoh immediately sent for Joseph, who explained that both of Pharaoh's dreams indicated that Egypt was about to have seven years of abundant crops followed by seven years of terrible famine. Pharaoh could see that Joseph's (God-given) insight was far superior to that of any of his other counselors, so he promoted Joseph to second in command over all of Egypt which including managing the food distribution and famine preparation (Genesis 41).

Years later, as the famine devastated the entire region, people from the surrounding areas all flocked to Egypt to get grain . . . including Joseph's brothers from Canaan. He knew who they were immediately, but they didn't recognize him with his new Egyptian fashion sense. Besides, it had been twenty years. Before revealing his identity, Joseph put them through some tests to see if they were still the same merciless group that had treated him so badly, or if they had more compassion toward their new younger brother, Benjamin. They passed all his tests, yet were quite terrified when they found out the Egyptian CEO they'd been doing business with was none other than their brother Joseph. As they bowed before him, Joseph realized his dreams as a teenager had finally come to pass. He assured them, "Do not be distressed and do not be angry with yourselves for selling me here, because it was to save lives that God sent me ahead of you. . . . God sent me ahead of you to preserve for you a remnant on earth and to save your lives by a great deliverance" (Genesis 45:5, 7).

Still, they feared Joseph's retribution, so he continued to try to persuade them, "Don't be afraid. Am I in the place of God? You intended to harm me, but God intended it for good to accomplish what is now being done, the saving of many lives. So then, don't be afraid. I will provide for you and your children" (Genesis 50:19-21).

In other words, Joseph could see clearly that God had orchestrated his whole life. Joseph now had a wife and two sons of his own. Soon his family in Canaan would join him on some prime real estate in Egypt, and they would all see God's bigger plan for all the wildernesses and distractions they had endured.

God has chosen believers to be people of divine destiny. Those who are built different acknowledge their positions and can remain optimistic like Joseph when circumstances turn grim. Because they know their identity, they can do more than just survive; they can thrive amid webs of deception and pits of rejection, slavery, and false accusation. God will never give up on us, and we must learn to never give up on Him!

Trust God in every season of your life—especially the ones that are dark, difficult, or disturbing. Believe that the plans He has for you are far greater than you could ever imagine. You will arrive at your destiny if you remain dependent on Him.

PERSEVERANCE AND PERSISTENCE ARE KEY

Some people do a good job of persevering through the difficult and challenging phases of life. In fact, it's the challenge of it all that keeps them focused. But what eventually throws them off-track and causes them to miss God's best for their lives is not the difficulty of life, but *comfort and convenience!* We like fast food, easy answers, and the path of least resistance. We need to remember that the things in this life that have any value *all come with a cost.*

Accomplishing anything meaningful in this life will be difficult. At times, it may flat-out be painful and uncomfortable. It may cost you some friends. It may hurt your reputation in certain circles of influence. It may be unpopular. But none of those realities means it's not worth it. Just because something is hard doesn't mean it's time to give up, give in, or settle. We must push through and first achieve the positive change we are looking for, and then sustain and maintain it.

In the counseling profession, there is a very important concept known as the Change Continuum. Within this continuum, James Prochaska, Carlo DiClemente, and John Norcross propose that there are five stages within the change cycle including:

> *Precontemplation*: When an individual does not yet acknowledge his/her problem and or need to change;

> *Contemplation*: When an individual acknowledges his/her problem, but is not yet ready or sure of wanting to make a change;

> *Preparation*: The stage where an individual is getting ready or preparing to make a change;

> *Action*: The stage where an individual implements the changing behavior to attain his/her goal; and

> *Maintenance*: The stage where the individual focuses on sustaining his/her work and efforts in pursuing the desired goal.

Sometimes a sixth stage is added—either *termination*, where the person has mastered the change, or *relapse*, where the person reverts to the behavior he/she had attempted to change.[40]

I've always liked how Norcross breaks the maintenance stage down, as he defines it with two words: *perseverance* and *persistence*. Sadly, when many people hit a certain point of challenge, adversity, or unfamiliarity, their first instinct is to *retreat*! It isn't that they aren't capable of pushing themselves past their limitations, it's just that they're reluctant to cross that line of discomfort. We must never forget that anything worth value in this life is going to come at a cost.

We can choose to reinvent ourselves by raising the bar every day to build, sharpen, and expand the pursuit of our goals. And we must be willing to persevere when the going gets tough. One of my favorite quotes is, "You will not find toughness in a comfortable environment."[41]

At times you will be discouraged and disappointed, and sometimes you may even feel defeated, but as long as you have breath in your lungs, God is not done with you yet. Keep pushing and keep fighting. Why? Because somebody may be depending on the decisions you make and the habits you create today, and that somebody just might be you.

FOURTEEN

HOW A LEGACY IS BORN

"I always figured there is no use being the richest man
in the cemetery. You cannot operate from there."

— Colonel Sanders

In 1952 at the age of 65, when most people are ready to slow down
and retire, Harland David Sanders began Kentucky Fried Chicken. His father died when he was six, and his mother had to work to
support the family. He was the oldest child, so his mother taught
him how to do the cooking to help take care of his siblings. By age
7, he had learned to cook an assortment of regional dishes.

After a stint in the army and failing to find success at several different jobs, at age 40 he started cooking for travelers going
through Corbin, Kentucky. Working out of a service station, but
with no restaurant attached, he served customers at his own dining room table. As interest in his cooking grew, he moved to a
motel/restaurant with seating for 142 people. For the next decade
he experimented with his recipes, and eventually landed on the
renowned "eleven herbs and spices" that still comprise his secret
blend. It's also when he discovered that his chicken tasted best and

cooked fastest when fried in a pressure cooker—another technique still used today.

He found himself bankrupt at the age of 65, with only his $105 monthly Social Security check for income. He went into chicken franchising, driving around the country cooking chicken for restaurant owners and their employees to sample. His recipe was rejected more than a thousand times before anyone accepted it.[42] But for those who liked it, he used handshake deals to authorize them to use his cooking techniques and secret formula in exchange for a nickel for every piece of chicken sold. A dozen years later, Kentucky Fried Chicken had more than 600 franchises, so he sold his interest in the business for $2 million, but "Colonel Sanders" long remained the face of the company.[43]

This story isn't just about business success; it's a challenge to live a life of significance. Harland Sanders demonstrates that it's never too late to begin again and make your life count for a purpose bigger than yourself. And it is safe to say that Colonel Sanders was built different. Even at rock-bottom and seeing little reason for hope, he never gave up hope. Sometimes being broken is the best place to be if you are yielded to God.

LIVING FOR A LEGACY

A hundred years from now, nobody is likely to know Zach Clinton's name, other than immediate family members. My fellow members of Generation Z will be only a historical footnote by then. Still, I want to leave a legacy—to make a difference while I'm here. I'm reminded of what one of my coaches once told us: "When you graduate from Liberty University, we will still have a baseball team. The program doesn't stop just because you are gone. So, how are you going to make your time here count? How do you want to be remembered?"

Legacies are rooted in consistency. When it comes to college football, no other team comes close to Alabama's legacy. People say that after a championship year, Alabama doesn't rebuild, they *reload*. When one group of champion players leave, another group is waiting in the wings to step up and take their place. Alabama is a team that opposing fans (myself included) love to hate because they are so good.

It may be that nobody is going to remember Zach Clinton's name, yet my legacy can certainly live on. Yours can, too. In time this book will turn to dust, but if it touches a single soul, that touches another soul, that touches another soul, it lives on. That's how the kingdom of God works. It's about consistently bringing honor and glory to Christ by touching souls, serving and loving those that God brings into our lives, and pouring into them something of eternal value that they can pass on. You might be saying, "But Zach, you don't understand. It's too late for me. I've blown it too many times. I've ruined my life." God specializes in resurrecting and restoring life and hope, even in situations that appear to be flat-lining. If you are still living, God can still work, if you let Him. Stop trying to limit a God who delights in impossibility.

God is calling you to something bigger than yourself, and it is in His calling that you will find ultimate fulfillment and peace. Some are called to be missionaries in far-off locales; others serve and influence family members and others in their circle. You may feel irrelevant at times, but your life and what you are doing is not.

I love this quote from Craig Groeschel:

So who do you want to become? I want to become someone who is faithful. But I'm always tempted to want to become someone other people think is important. I struggle with wanting others to view me as important for being successful or a good author or the pastor of a thriving church or a popular podcast host.

God did not call me to be important. When I get to heaven, God will not say, "Well done, my good and important servant." No, he didn't call me to be important. He called me to be faithful.

What's interesting is when I aim for the target of faithful, I end up doing what's truly important.[44]

I love that last line. That's how a legacy is born. When you stand before Jesus, will He say, "Well done, my good and *faithful* servant"?

In this world you will have trouble. Jesus warned us we would (John 16:33). All of us are going to experience tough times, and sometimes we all fall short of the glory of God. But amid tough times, we can be committed to the process, committed to the pursuit of obedience which leads to Christlikeness. We live in a world that preaches perfection, but God is all about the process. "Being confident of this," wrote Paul, "that he who began a good work in you will carry it on to completion until the day of Christ Jesus" (Philippians 1:6). The question is, are you confident that God is working in you to finish the process? We must allow Him to work through us.

PURSUIT OVER PERFECTION

Tony Robbins once asked Michael Jordan in an interview, "What makes you the best in the world? Is it skill? Is it talent? Is it abilities? Is it background? Is it training?" Jordan responded, "Tony, I can tell you the truth and it won't sound like false modesty.

I didn't even make the high school basketball team, sophomore year. I was cut. What it is, is every day I demand more from myself than anybody else could possibly expect. I don't compete with other people. I compete with what I'm capable of."[45]

Kobe Bryant was asked a similar question at the end of his career about what made him one of the greatest to ever play the game. His response: "What I'm doing right now, I'm chasing perfection . . . and if I don't get it, I'm going to get this close."[46]

The most elite teams and athletes I've ever worked with understand that success is not about competing with other people. Many athletes get lost in trash talking and one-upmanship, but the greats understand that the only meaningful competition is competing with themselves.

Too many of us have been misled by the old saying, "Practice makes perfect." The truth is, practice doesn't make perfect, but practice *does* make progress. We need to understand that perfection is unattainable and instead throw ourselves into simply showing up and giving our all.

God doesn't expect us to be perfect, but He asks us to be obedient because obedience leads to Christlikeness—and I'd much rather pursue the Lord and spend my life becoming more like Jesus than spend my life worrying about meeting anyone else's expectations of me. Faithfulness and pursuit of Jesus leads to love, joy, peace, patience, kindness, goodness, faithfulness, gentleness, and self-control. That sounds like fun. That sounds exciting. That sounds invigorating. I'll take the fruit of the Spirit over any title, promotion, or raise any day of the week.

And when you're obedient to God, you never know what might happen. You've probably never heard of Roy Brunson, but his legacy is changing the world. Brunson was a vice-president of a *Fortune* 500 company, a multimillionaire, and a hardcore atheist since childhood. His mother had drilled into him that a God who allowed evil in the world couldn't possibly exist. But one day Roy's glorious life came crashing down. I'll spare you the details, but he found himself broke, devastated, and angry. In fact, he had bottomed out and had a plan to commit suicide after his plane landed in Memphis. But God had other plans for Roy. Listen to Roy's own words:

I was on a plane from Dallas to Memphis, contemplating how I would take my own life, when an attractive, middle-aged woman sat next to me. After some small talk, she could tell something was bothering me.

"Jesus loves you," she said with a warm smile.

"Lady," I shouted back, "exactly what did God do for you anyway?"

That was a mistake. She told me she had been totally blind for over thirteen years. One night after coming home from visiting relatives, her husband, who was a Baptist minister, got down on his knees and started praying for her eyesight while she lay in bed. She said he prayed, "God, I know that you can make Marolyn see. O God, make her see now," and just like that she saw her husband Acie for the first time. Then she saw her daughter for the first time. She had met and married Acie while she was in college when she was blind. She then went on to explain that she had numerous doctors examine her and they all said it was impossible for her to see. The damage to her eyes was still there and beyond repair. But they could not explain how she now had 20/20 vision. They had to admit that the only explanation possible was a supernatural one. It could only be a miracle.

Her blue eyes looked right through me into my soul. I was very frightened. Could my mother be wrong? Was there really a God that loved me and had a plan for my life?[47]

Roy Brunson left that plane a new man, completely born again and set on a new God-directed path. God called him, using Isaiah 6:8-9:

"Then I heard the voice of the Lord saying, 'Whom shall I send? And who will go for us?' And I said, 'Here am I. Send Me!'

[God] said, 'Go and tell this people . . .'"

That was in 1987. Since then, Roy answered that call to the mission field by founding Worldlight Ministries and leading thirty crusades in Ukraine and four in Kenya. He started orphanages for handicapped children that provided food, clothing, washing machines, toilets, and showers. He also worked with hospitals and prisons in both of those countries. Before Roy passed, he had led over 215,000 people to faith in Christ.

God uses executives, missionaries, and fried chicken salesmen. He takes what's in our hands and builds a legacy. What's in *your* hand?

FIFTEEN

UNASHAMED

"Out of 100 men, one will read the Bible,
the other 99 will read the Christian."

— **D.L. Moody**

Amal was a teenage Arab girl in the Middle East when she first heard about Jesus. After expressing interest in seeking Him further, one of her high school teachers urged her not to, warning her that she could be killed. Yet she was unable to shake her desire to know more. Raised Muslim, Amal had not read the Bible because it was forbidden in her home.

Struggling for answers, she cried out in prayer, "Okay, God, I want to ask you if you are the god of Islam. Just tell me that you are, and I will wear the hijab [head covering] and do all the prayers you want. But if you are the God of Christians, even if this will lead me to be killed, I will still believe in you." God answered her prayer in a dream. Listen to Amal's own words.

In my dream, I woke up. There was so much light I couldn't look at it. The light, who I later realized was Jesus, told me to start walking. Every time I fell, he would grab my hand, pull me up, and continue walking. We reached an oasis. He asked me to grab a book out of the water. He said, "The answer you are looking for is inside that book." I read the verse where it says, "I am the way and the truth and the life."

When she woke up, Amal pondered the comforting, guiding presence of the light and the strange words she had read. Having not heard them before, she questioned if they were from the Quran, the Bible, or somewhere else. Her research led her to John 14:6, where Jesus spoke those exact words, "I am the way and the truth and the life. No one comes to the Father except through me."

Amal was good to her word. She immediately gave her life to Jesus and began living out her faith *unashamedly* in front of her family, friends, and culture. God has protected her, and she has needed it often. On numerous occasions her family confiscated her Bibles and burned them. She's been beaten by her brother and father. Her life has been repeatedly threatened. She was locked in her room for two weeks with no cell phone, and little food and water. Twice during that time, she fainted, yet she never wavered in her faith. "I wanted to be like a testimony and prove that I am God's daughter," she said.

Despite the violent reaction to her faith from her family and community, Amal has continued to courageously live out her convictions in front of them. As a result, she has led three of her sisters and her younger brother to Jesus. She is having an impact on the culture around her, even leading a group who converted from Islam to Christianity. She's authentic and unashamed, with an "even if . . ." mindset. Even if her family rejects her . . . even if she is shunned by her community . . . even if the threats on her life persist . . . Amal remains faithful to the "God of Christians" who revealed himself to her.[48]

A LONG HISTORY OF CANCEL CULTURE

Few of us in the West experience a level of opposition to our faith that Amal has to endure, although rejection of Christian morals and standards seems to be growing. You've heard the stories. A high school football coach gets sidelined because he led his team in prayer. A politician is marginalized and called hateful for embracing the Bible as the inspired Word of God. A science professor is denied tenure because he's a Christian. A pro football player is reprimanded by the NFL for kneeling in prayer after a touchdown, even as another is praised for his courage to kneel in protest during the National Anthem.

It's not that our culture minds your faith; they just want you to stay quiet about it. Keep it in your little Christian world, just don't go public with it. If you do, the cancel culture is right there to shame and silence you, to put you back where they think you belong. Yet if you are built different, some things are simply nonnegotiable.

And the opponents to Christianity know the truth: when men and women live out their faith unashamedly with integrity, they impact their culture deeply. Bold examples of faith and obedience to God influence individuals, families, organizations, teams, schools, and nations. We've seen many biblical examples in this book so far, and this chapter will provide a couple more.

Daniel was a man of exceptional qualities and upright character. He had been taken into exile by the Babylonians because they noticed he was built different, chosen with some other Hebrews because he was "without any physical defect, handsome, showing aptitude for every kind of learning, well informed, quick to understand, and qualified to serve in the king's palace" (Daniel 1:4). In Babylon, he had been enrolled in a three-year leadership training program where he excelled (along with Shadrach, Meshach, and Abednego). They proved to be "ten times better than all the magicians and enchanters in [Nebuchadnezzar's] whole kingdom" (Daniel 1:20). And for many years, Daniel served a series of Babylonian kings.

In time, the Persians defeated the Babylonians and brought their own cabinet of officials, but by then, Daniel's reputation was apparently so established that Persian king Darius made Daniel one of three administrators over all the other 120 rulers across the kingdom. In fact, Darius was intending to set Daniel over the entire kingdom (Daniel 6:1-3). Of course, those other leaders weren't happy about Daniel's impending promotion. Politics wasn't much different then from what it is now, so the other 122 immediately tried to find something on Daniel they could use to bring him down, "but they could find no corruption in him, because he was trustworthy and neither corrupt nor negligent" (Daniel 6:4).

Daniel's opponents knew he was a man of God because he had been living his faith unashamedly and publicly before them. When they couldn't find anything else to accuse him of, they went after his faith and tried to cancel him. They played to Darius's ego, and convinced him to sign a new *unchangeable* law that proclaimed the King the only figure his people could pray to for the next thirty days. And their edict included a built-in penalty: all offenders would be thrown into the lions' den (Daniel 6:6-8). Essentially, this was attempted, premeditated murder. Daniel's critics knew all along that he wouldn't stop praying because of any law.

Not much has changed in the past 2,500 years. Critics still want to prevent people of faith from being anywhere they can wield their influence. They work incredibly hard and passionately to silence Christian voices in one way or another. That's what these people do. Refusing to give in to cultural pressure will often cost you. Occasionally, it will cost you everything.

Caught up in the emotion of the moment, King Darius signed the law, and the 120 schemers went into action, tailing Daniel and staking out his house. What were Daniel's options? It would have been little trouble for him to lie low for thirty days and not make waves. He could have closed his curtains and prayed silently. He could have taken a vacation. Yet Daniel did what he always did. He didn't freak out, try to defend himself, or adjust his behavior. He wasn't arrogant, but he remained quietly confident, knowing full well they were watching as he continued to pray and practice his faith openly and out loud.

Those who are built different know the cost of not compromising, yet they realize the cost of compromise is infinitely greater. To them, there's no choice. So when Daniel made a point to pray in the open, his opponents caught him red-handed and ran to the king to tattle on him. Darius was distressed and frustrated that he'd been played, but his hands were tied. Daniel was bound for the lions' den.

Amazingly, King Darius expressed hope in Daniel's God even as he was ordering Daniel to be thrown in: "May your God, whom you serve continually, rescue you!" It was a sleepless night for Darius, and one without food or entertainment. Apparently, Daniel's night was much better. As soon as it was light, Darius rushed to the lions' den to check on Daniel. He was overjoyed to hear Daniel say, "May the king live forever! My God sent his angel, and he shut the mouths of the lions. They have not hurt me, because I was found innocent in his sight. Nor have I ever done any wrong before you, Your Majesty" (Daniel 6:21-22).

So for Daniel, the story has a happy ending. He got his promotion and he continued to prosper during the reign of Darius and Cyrus the Persian (Daniel 6:28). His accusers, on the other hand, were thrown into the lion's den . . . along with their families. Apparently, it was Persian custom to execute the families of convicted criminals along with the actual criminals.[49] And they didn't fare as well as Daniel.

Secular culture can be dark when sin and wickedness rule. It was for Daniel, and it can be for us at times. But Daniel was a light in that darkness. He was built differently. Is it possible that God is asking you to walk through your dark night so others can see the light of God shine from you? When you are built different, it's possible to thrive in the darkness. Our world needs more Daniels (and "Danielles," like Amal) today.

An old quote often attributed to Dr. Seuss is, "Why fit in when you were born to stand out?" I think that would have been an appropriate motto for Daniel's life. Like Daniel, I want to be remembered as someone who was *unashamed*. What about you?

PRAISE BEFORE YOUR BREAKTHROUGH

During the hardest seasons of my life, I am drawn to the book of James where the author reminds us to "Consider it pure joy, my brothers and sisters, whenever you face trials of many kinds" (James 1:2). Sometimes we need to realize that our wilderness seasons, no matter how long or hard or dry they may seem, are catalysts for growth and life. If you don't give up, your hardest seasons can become your harvest seasons!

Paul and Silas exemplified this when they were tossed into prison. They weren't thrown into the county jail for a few hours. They were taken into the "inner" prison—the deepest, darkest, nastiest part of a dungeon. Very little light got in, and the only sounds were likely groaning prisoners and squealing rats. Their feet were placed in stocks—restraining devices locked around their feet that kept them from moving. So not only were Paul and Silas in the deepest dungeon, but they were also in bodily confinement with no idea how long they would be there.

How would you have responded in their place? So imagine the other prisoners' surprise when Paul and Silas began singing praises and worshiping God. They had every reason to whine, complain, or collapse in fear. Yet they worshiped in this dark, miserable place in the face of death. And as their voices rose in praise, their circumstances began to change. The ground began to tremble and the prison began to shake. Miraculously, all the prisoners' stocks snapped, their chains fell off, and their cell doors opened.

Roman authorities didn't look favorably on guards who let their prisoners escape, so the jailer was going to kill himself . . . until Paul stopped him. Another miracle: none of the prisoners left. Instead of escaping, there was a revival. The jailer called for lights to be brought in, and then pleaded to Paul and Silas, "What must I do to be saved?" Paul explained to him the simple truth of the gospel, and the jailer and his whole household believed. Your prison is your opportunity to worship your way to breakthrough.

God came through for Paul and Silas in a big way when they chose the pathway of praise. God responds to praise because it is impossible to praise Him while we're whining. Praise amid difficultly shows trust in the living God. Who knows? Maybe your prison is only a temporary holding cell, giving you an opportunity to worship and receive the freedom that only He can provide.

Individuals who are built different understand that they must learn to be faithful wherever they are. As Paul wrote, "I have learned to be content whatever the circumstances" (Philippians 4:11). Gratitude, praise, and contentment aren't always instinctive responses, so we must be intentional about recognizing opportunities to implement them within our daily lives. Every difficult situation is a *choice* to *rejoice*. Look for opportunities to worship and give thanks in your wilderness. When you do, you are setting yourself up for a breakthrough.

SIXTEEN

PICK UP YOUR MAT!

"Disappointment is inevitable. But to become
discouraged, is a choice I make."

— Charles Stanley

've said a lot so far about what we need to do as believers to improve our spiritual lives—to be built differently and to have an "even if . . ." mindset anytime things go wrong. But it's quite harmful, if not dangerous, to forget that sometimes we get into situations that only God can handle. In fact, sometimes God leads us into circumstances that we can't handle on our own just to show us that He *can*.

One such example was when the Israelites were finally leaving Egypt and came upon the Red Sea. It looked like Pharaoh's army had them trapped, and the people were absolutely panicked. They were all set to turn around, beg forgiveness from the Egyptians, and go back to slavery. Yet God had led them to that specific spot at that specific time using an unmistakable pillar of cloud/fire to direct them.

Moses tried to assure them, "Do not be afraid. Stand firm and you will see the deliverance the Lord will bring you today. The

Egyptians you see today you will never see again. The Lord will fight for you; you need only to be still" (Exodus 14:13-14). Then God did what the people couldn't do for themselves: the Red Sea parted and they walked across on dry land while the Egyptian chariot wheels jammed up and held them in place until the Red Sea waters poured back down and drowned them.

Then, when everyone was safely on the other side of the Sea and the threat was gone, God gave the people laws and spelled out His expectations for them. When God acts, we can (and should) respond. But if we get impatient and start trying to do God's job for Him, we can create unnecessary problems.

After God had promised to provide a child to Abraham and Sarah, they waited for a long while, but then began to become anxious. First Abraham tried to designate his most trusted servant to be his heir. But God again assured him his heir would be his own flesh and blood, and then made a covenant with Abraham to confirm it (Genesis 15). But later, Sarah's frustration over her childlessness caused her to take matters into her own hands and suggested that Abraham sleep with her handmaid, Hagar. The result was Ishmael, a child that immediately created dissension within their household (Genesis 16; 21:8-21), and continues to create conflict between Arabs (Ishmael's descendants) and Jews (Isaac's descendants).

God waited until Abraham and Sarah had given up hope that *they* could ever have a child (what were the odds when she was 89 and he was 99?), and then proved that *He* could still make it happen. Sarah had a child in her old age (Genesis 21:1-7), just as Mary would later have a child despite her virginity (Luke 1:26-38). The Lord wants us to really believe that "with God all things are possible" (Matthew 19:26).

People who are built different . . . those with an "even if . . ." mindset, learn to discern which situations they need to wait out a little longer until God makes His will clear(er), and which ones they need to tackle right away. They learn to determine if they should stay in their wilderness a while longer, or if it's time to move on and get busy with God's purpose for their lives. Such decisions are rarely instinctive. It's always preferable to have clear direction, one way or another.

Waiting on the Lord can be one of the most difficult challenges for those of us who are go-getter, type-A individuals, chomping at the bit to get out and do God's work. But before God will work *through* us, He wants to work *in* us, and that often requires waiting.

Not long ago, I interviewed Richie McKay, the head basketball coach at Liberty University. He carries a contagious spirit that draws people in and ignites them. Something I took away from our interview was how Coach shared that from his experience, when someone is disappointed, discouraged, or disengaged, it usually comes from one of three things: (1) Their own sin; (2) Another person's sin against them; or (3) Unmet expectations.

I think we've said enough already about personal sin and the offenses against us that require forgiveness. In review, it's critical to receive God's forgiveness and then forgive ourselves so we can get unstuck and move forward in life. This same principle must be applied equally to others when they sin against us. Just as God's ever-flowing, never-ending grace and forgiveness are gifts that we can't possibly comprehend, our ability to forgive others is also bigger than ourselves. It requires the supernatural power of God moving through us to acquire the grace to give grace.

C.S. Lewis wrote:

To be a Christian means to forgive the inexcusable, because God has forgiven the inexcusable in you. This is hard. It is perhaps not so hard to forgive a single great injury. But to

forgive the incessant provocations of daily life—to keep on forgiving the bossy mother-in-law, the bullying husband, the nagging wife, the selfish daughter, the deceitful son—how can we do it? Only, I think, by remembering where we stand, by meaning our words when we say in our prayers each night "forgive us our trespasses as we forgive those that trespass against us." We are offered forgiveness on no other terms. To refuse it is to refuse God's mercy for ourselves. There is no hint of exceptions and God means what He says.[50]

Of course, only the power of God can enable us to practice the level of forgiveness that Lewis describes. Until we allow God to empower us to forgive those who have failed us, we will remain stuck, and eventually our unforgiveness will become bitter poison. It will waste our souls away and infect everyone else we interact with.

UNMET EXPECTATIONS

Let's now turn our attention to the third of Coach McKay's reasons we experience disappointment and discouragement, which is *unmet expectations*. How often do you throw up your hands to quit, erupt in anger, or maybe weep when your sure-fire plans or rock-solid expectations crumble before your eyes . . . when someone you depended on lets you down . . . when disaster comes out of nowhere and puts you in a life situation you didn't expect or ask for? Sometimes we get disappointed when God doesn't give us more than we need, or He holds us back for a season, maybe a very long season. When that happens, do you trust that God knows something you don't and has your best interest in mind? Personally, I believe that God gives us exactly what we need for the moment, because if He were to give us more than that, we might not turn to Him or fully rely on Him anymore.

"Give me neither poverty nor riches," says a proverb, "but give me only my daily bread. Otherwise, I may have too much and disown you and say, 'Who is the Lord?' Or I may become poor and steal, and so dishonor the name of my God" (Proverbs 30:8-9). The apostle Paul put it this way: "I have learned to be content whatever the circumstances. I know what it is to be in need, and I know what it is to have plenty. I have learned the secret of being content in any and every situation, whether well fed or hungry, whether living in plenty or in want. I can do all this through him who gives me strength" (Philippians 4:11-13).

This makes me think of the manna that God provided for the Israelites as they were wandering in the desert. Though the Promised Land would be their ultimate destiny, in the meantime, God never gave them more than they needed on any given day. We ought to appreciate that daily miracle of His showing up every day to provide just what we need. It could be the physical or emotional ability to walk and not grow weary. Sometimes it may be the strength to stand firm in trying times. It could be His provision of peace that passes understanding, meeting a practical need, or a bit of Holy Spirit's wisdom to complete a difficult job. Let God come through in unique ways, showing up in your pain, disappointment, and in more of your everyday moments.

We should be more content with small victories that keep us moving toward our Promised Land. We need to stop looking for the big wins, and rather celebrate the small but significant victories of receiving God's grace in the moments we need it most. Too often, people get mired in discouragement or disappointment because they set the bar too high and then fail. Many give up at that point and don't finish what they started.

We must learn to be still and know God is in control. The Spirit of God often speaks in a still small whisper, which we miss altogether unless we press in closer to Him and His Word. And even if

God seems silent, and you feel distanced from or disappointed in Him, that doesn't mean that He is absent.

It is critical during this process that we stay connected to the source. "I am the vine; you are the branches," said Jesus. "If you remain in me and I in you, you will bear much fruit; apart from me you can do nothing" (John 15:5). When you're walking through the woods and come upon a limb that's just lying there, it is usually dead or in the process of dying. Once it becomes disconnected from its tree or vine, it no longer produces fruit and is only good for firewood. A lot of Christians attempt to function apart from the vine, and then wonder why they are withering and drying up.

LET JESUS DO WIIAT ONLY HE CAN DO

Again, we only hurt ourselves when we try to do things ourselves that only Jesus can do. I think of the man at the pool of Bethesda in John 5. He had gone through *thirty-eight years* of his life unable to walk. He stayed by the pool in hopes of being first into the water when the time was right, but someone who can't walk can't make a mad dash for the water on cue. He was unable to help himself on his own, and he had no support system of friends to give him a hand. So when Jesus walked over to him one day and asked, "Do you want to get well?" his first response was to make excuses for why he hadn't already resolved his own problem.

But Jesus didn't listen to the man's excuses. He was there to do for the man what he couldn't do for himself. He simply said, "Get up! Pick up your mat and walk" (John 15:8). And after being an invalid for thirty-eight years, the man immediately picked up his mat and started walking. His story is a prime example of why we should never give up on God.

As we wait for Jesus to do what only He can do in our lives, prayer is our lifeline to remain connected to the Source. Don't confuse prayer with some formal religious ritual we go through to get to God. Prayer is first and foremost a relationship with a person, Jesus. It is a way to come into His presence and abide in Him through fellowship and His word.

Jesus invited us into a relationship when He said, "Here I am! I stand at the door and knock. If anyone hears my voice and opens the door, I will come in and eat with that person, and they with me" (Revelation 3:20). Jesus wants to have fellowship with us, and it's through that fellowship that His life is imparted to us.

Charles Stanley observes: "Every time we pray to God, seeking His will, there are two things He wants to show us. He wants to show us Himself, and He wants to show us what He is able to do. Is there anything greater than seeking God and knowing His power?"[51]

Then, after connecting with God through prayer, and after Jesus does for us the things that only He can do, we put the things He is teaching us into practice. James affirmed this when he said, "Do not merely listen to the word, and so deceive yourselves. Do what it says. Anyone who listens to the word but does not do what it says is like someone who looks at his face in a mirror and, after looking at himself, goes away and immediately forgets what he looks like" (James 1:22-24).

Maybe you're biding your time in the wilderness, learning what God wants you to discover there. But when God does what only He can do, it's time for action. One action God always calls us to is increasing our faith. Have you been incapacitated by fear, laziness, or some other obstacle lately? If so, perhaps the time has come to "pick up your mat and walk."

Keep in step with God's Spirit (Galatians 5:25). If God has placed you in the wilderness, don't rush back to normal life too soon. Slow down until you find out what you need to learn. But after you do, get up and get going. Some people become so sedate that their spiritual muscles begin to atrophy. But if we're properly waiting for God, that won't be a problem. Waiting actually makes us stronger! Remember Isaiah's promise:

> **Do you not know? Have you not heard?**
> **The Lord is the everlasting God, the Creator of the ends of the earth.**
> **He will not grow tired or weary, and his understanding no one can fathom.**
> **He gives strength to the weary and increases the power of the weak.**
> **Even youths grow tired and weary, and young men stumble and fall;**
> **but those who hope in [wait upon] the Lord will renew their strength.**
> **They will soar on wings like eagles;**
> **they will run and not grow weary,**
> **they will walk and not be faint.**
> **(Isaiah 40:28-31)**

So wait upon the Lord. Renew your energy. Learn to walk . . . or run . . . or even soar. And then, in the next chapter, we'll look at another source of strength available to you.

SEVENTEEN

FRIENDS THROUGH THE FIRE

"I used to want to fix people,
but now I just want to be with them."

— Bob Goff

So far, we've talked about many qualities of those who are built different, who have that all-important "even if . . ." mindset, faith, and endurance. Those qualities include humility, honor, honesty, selflessness, loyalty, respect, gratefulness, grace, love, authenticity, courage, and others. We may not have mastered them all, but that's what we're striving for.

Another quality that we need to add to the list, however, is "others-centered." As built-different people grow into the individuals God created them to be, the more they see their lives in the context of others. Rick Warren wrote (although his comment is often misattributed to C.S. Lewis): "This is true humility: not thinking less of ourselves but thinking of ourselves *less*."[52]

Any of us who are truly serious about discovering God's purpose for our lives are going to quickly realize our purpose has something to do with helping other people. The better we connect with the church, the body of Christ, the more effective will be our ministries. And those connections must be authentic and ongoing because many of us tend to isolate in our own little worlds, physically and/or emotionally, whenever something goes wrong. It's possible to be in a crowd and still be detached, with walls erected to keep others out.

How many spouses live under the same roof, yet are miles apart, emotionally? Satan knows that even though we isolate to try to minimize our disappointments and discouragement, isolation *intensifies* them. As Charles Spurgeon said, "Satan always hates Christian fellowship; it is his policy to keep Christians apart. Anything which can divide saints from one another he delights in. He attaches far more importance to godly intercourse than we do."[53]

If the enemy can get us alone, he can pummel us with his lies. His strategy is "divide and conquer." He found Eve when she was alone and confused her with half-truths and enticements. Chances are, if Adam had been present, the serpent's power of deceit and persuasion would have been greatly reduced.

PEOPLE FUEL MATTERS

In the mental health space, we often use the term "people fuel" to describe the significance and power that can be found in relationship. I believe God often uses people as conduits through which He channels His messages of hope, grace, encouragement, and motivation to a hurting and broken world. While it is true that standing with God sometimes means standing alone, that's altogether different from being a loner.

David stood alone for God when he fought Goliath, but at other times he gained much strength and courage from his deep friendships, notably with King Saul's son, Jonathan. When David needed a trusted ally inside Saul's household, God sent him Jonathan, a brother-like comrade who had his back on numerous occasions, even defying his own father to save David's life (1 Samuel 20). They couldn't have been closer friends: "Jonathan became one in spirit with David, and he loved him as himself" (1 Samuel 18:1). We all need a Jonathan in our lives, an "even if . . ." friend who stands beside us no matter what we're going through.

God gives us extra-strength relationships to help us through life's most trying moments. When God wants to promote you, provide for you, or protect you, He quite often does so through a person. It never occurred to David to manipulate or use Jonathan to advance his purposes. The two genuinely loved each other with a pure, godly, brotherly love. Jonathan and David epitomized loving others as yourself (1 Samuel 18:3). Years later, after Jonathan's tragic death and David eventually became king, David would honor their covenant by searching out Jonathan's lame son, Mephibosheth, and making him part of the royal family. When David needed extra support, God sent Jonathan; when Jonathan's son needed a breakthrough, God sent David.

From the beginning, God designed people to need close relationships. After God created Adam, He said, "It is not good for the man to be alone" (Genesis 2:18). Our first thought when reading this passage may be that God created Eve as Adam's partner/helpmate and for procreation of the species, which is true, yet it goes much further than that. It is not good for any human being to be alone, period. We were made to be in relationship with God first, and then with a spouse, and then with a community of believers.

These relationships are emphasized when Scripture describes the church as the *body* of Christ. Each member is designed with a different combination of gifts to address different functions, just as the varied parts and organs of a human body have their specific purpose. Likewise, each part is dependent on the gifts and abilities of others for good health and the ability to grow in Christlikeness to fulfill our callings (1 Corinthians 12:12-27). Without all those other members imparting their gifts into us, we will never reach our full potential. This pierces the prideful heart that says, "I don't need anyone! I'm my own man (or woman)." Nonetheless, it is God's way.

When I was growing up, my dad and I liked to watch episodes of *Wild Kingdom*. It was fascinating to watch lions stalking their prey. Their tactic was to isolate. They didn't go after the whole herd of gazelles or antelope. They'd use their roar to induce such fear that it caused the herd to scatter and separate from each other, then they would zero in on ones that were isolated and farthest from the rest. Once its victim was weary and wandering, the lion pounced. Countless times when the lions came on, Dad slipped in a little Bible lesson, quoting 1 Peter 5:8: "Be alert and of sober mind. Your enemy the devil prowls around like a roaring lion looking for someone to devour."

Fear will cause us to pull away from each other into our own little holes, into our own little ruts, into our own little patterns until we begin to believe that nobody cares. The enemy of our souls roars into our situations, hoping to startle and isolate us. That is why the author of Hebrews warns us with urgency: "Let us consider how we may spur one another on toward love and good deeds, not giving up meeting together, as some are in the habit of doing, but encouraging one another—and all the more as you see the Day approaching" (Hebrews 10:24-25). The more world events around us intensify, the more we need each other. The more our personal lives intensify, the more we need others to encourage us in the fight.

Back in Chapter 12, we covered Paul's shipwreck on Malta and mentioned that he finally made it to Rome. But here I want to point out something that happened along the way. At this stage of his life, Paul had completed three long and intensive missionary journeys where he had been repeatedly persecuted, including beatings, death threats, and even a stoning (Acts 14:19). Nothing seemed to stop him. You may think that Paul's indomitable spirit meant he was a tough, stoic guy with no need for personal affirmation, which seems true to a point. Yet as he got closer to Rome, after all he had been through, he came upon some believers who invited him to spend a week, which must have been a welcome option for him. But as word spread that Paul was nearby, people came pouring out of neighboring towns and came from great distances to see him. Scripture simply says that "At the sight of these people Paul thanked God and was encouraged" (Acts 28:15), but surely it was one of the more emotional experiences of Paul's life.

Even a hardened traveler like Paul appreciated encouragement, and as he wrote letters to the various churches, he frequently singled out the individuals who had encouraged and supported him. Yes, we need each other. Personally, I want to become the best encourager I can be, because "encourage" literally means *to give courage to*. All I want to do with my life, including what I want to do with this book, is to instill encouragement in other people. I want to give them courage to see themselves, this world, their pain and difficulties, and their God from a perspective they've never seen before. That's what encouragement is.

Not long ago, I did research and filmed a video on suicidality—the risk of suicide by those with suicidal thoughts, who have a plan for how to do it, and may have already attempted it. Suicide has become a leading cause of death in the United States and is a complicated issue with many variables, including chemical and mental factors. One of the top contributors, however, is that people don't understand their value to others, their self-worth. The enemy used COVID-19 to isolate a whole society and exacerbate the problem, and suicide rates skyrocketed. When we isolate ourselves, it only reinforces the misbelief that nobody's there and that nobody cares.

We become distressed and vulnerable when relationships that were meant to encourage and heal us are somehow short-circuited. Sometimes we open ourselves up to others who wind up hurting us, so we isolate ourselves in the determination to never be susceptible to that kind of pain again.

Jesus understood what it was like to be hurt. He understood what it was like to be betrayed and to have people forsake Him. But at the end of the day, He responded with grace and mercy. As He was dying on the cross, He said, "Father, forgive them, for they do not know what they are doing" (Luke 23:34). Jesus understood the power and the significance of relationships.

There's an old saying that states the obvious, "If you see a turtle sitting on a fencepost, you can be sure someone put him there." An old African proverb advises, "If you want to go fast, go alone. But if you want to go far, go together." Life makes more sense when we acknowledge that other people enable us to go farther than we could ever go alone, and that when we're viewing the world from atop a fencepost, we couldn't have gotten there without a lot of help. Isaac Newton famously said, "If I have seen further it is by standing on the shoulders of Giants." Who are some of the giants in your life who came before you and made your life a bit less difficult than it might have been otherwise? Who are those who lift you up when you really need encouragement?

I think of my most painful moments. If it weren't for my friends, family, the members of my Bible study, and other people that God sent my way, I could have withdrawn into myself and made some poor choices instead of growing through those difficult experiences. Your environment impacts your experience. The people you surround yourself with will influence the trajectory of your life. Who are those people in your life? Are they constructive or destructive? Do they push you closer to your goals or pull you further away? Do they motivate you to become your best, or allow you to settle for less?

Sidney Portier wrote, "If you walk down the street and someone is with you, he'll adjust to your pace or you to his, and you'll never be aware of it. There's no effort. It simply happens. And the same thing can happen with the rhythm of your life."[54] Whose pace have you adjusted to?"

Some of us may need to take an inventory of the people we allow to speak into our lives. Too many of us seek community for validation rather than for teaching and correction. If someone *always* accepts you for who you are, perhaps he or she isn't the one assigned to help push you to where God has destined you to be.

One of the hardest lessons I've had to learn in my own life is that I can't give equal time to everyone who wants it. Not everyone helps me experience the fullness of what God has called me to, and some even inhibit it. It doesn't necessarily mean they're bad people or that I love them any less. It just means that sometimes following God's calling on my life requires taking a path they have no interest in.

I want to surround myself with people who will love, encourage, and uplift me, yet I also want them to push and sharpen me to be the best version of myself. Scripture addresses this:

> "As iron sharpens iron, so one person sharpens another" (Proverbs 27:17).

> "A friend loves at all times, and a brother is born for a time of adversity" (Proverbs 17:17).

> "Walk with the wise and become wise, for a companion of fools suffers harm" (Proverbs 13:20).

> "Do not be misled: 'Bad company corrupts good character'" (1 Corinthians 15:33).

> "Words from a friend can be trusted, but an enemy multiplies kisses" (Proverbs 27:6).

Great team cultures are built on understanding the significance of relationships, of family, and of having each other's backs. When groups of committed individuals unite behind a common goal, amazing things happen—whether on the playing field or in the church sanctuary.

WHEN THE HEAT IS ON

I want to circle back to a story I introduced in Chapter 1—the dramatic account of Shadrach, Meshach, and Abednego, the ones responsible for the title of this book. When threatened with death by fiery furnace and given one final chance to submit, they made their answer clear: "If we are thrown into the blazing furnace, the God we serve is able to deliver us from it, and he will deliver us from Your Majesty's hand. *But even if* he does not, we want you to know, Your Majesty, that we will not serve your gods or worship the image of gold you have set up" (Daniel 3:17-18, emphasis added).

Obviously, they had a deep commitment to the true, living God and He empowered them. Yet I suspect they also drew much courage from each other's commitments. And the point I really want to emphasize as this book winds down is the surprise ending. As Nebuchadnezzar stood watching in stunned fascination at the three of them casually walking around in the fire, he also saw a fourth figure who looked "like a son of the gods" (Daniel 3:25).

When you commit to being built differently, and to developing an "even if . . ." mindset in response to what God asks you to do, you may sometimes find yourself amid fiery trials . . . but *you will never find yourself alone.* Even if all your friends desert you, God never will. He will be with you before, during, and after you feel the heat. God not only gives us friends through the fire, but God is in the midst of the fire with us.

One of the greatest blessings we can possibly have is our relationships, because that's what we were created for—first and foremost with God, and then with those He places in our lives. Relationships are our opportunity to love, serve, and grow, even in the fire. That is why Satan loves to rupture them and keep us isolated.

I just want to help people understand that they don't have to be alone, that they need to press into relationships. As we do everything we possibly can to make the most of life, we need like-minded friends who will push us, challenge us, and come alongside us to offer safety and security.

Whether you're in the fiery furnaces, lions' dens, deepest pits, and bleak wildernesses of life, or just the trying times when everything feels dry and lifeless, Jesus is there with fresh life and hope—perhaps in the form of other people to infuse you with new enthusiasm. We need those battle buddies to remind us that we are never alone. No matter what you're going through in this season of life, I encourage you to recruit trustworthy friends to go with you through the fire.

EIGHTEEN

PUSHING TOWARD THE MARK

"If God only used perfect people,
nothing would ever get done."

— Rick Warren

In this final chapter about what it means to have an "even if . . ." mindset, I want to remind you of a quote I shared with you toward the beginning of this book: "You don't have to win all your fights, but you must fight all your fights."[55] I hope by this point you've discovered the wonderful news that as men and women with the Spirit of God inside us, we can enjoy the victory He has already won. Anchored by God's abundant grace and gift of salvation, our job is simply to choose every day to be an active participant in the story God is writing for our lives. I often reflect on a quote that's most often attributed to Woody Allen: "90% of success is just showing up." I believe that if you show up every day with that "even if . . ." mindset, God will faithfully take you the rest of the way.

A few years ago, I came across a fascinating story I want to share with you. A woman who had been diagnosed with a terminal illness was given only about six months to live. She met with her pastor to discuss some of her final wishes: what songs she wanted sung at her funeral and what Scriptures she wanted read. Then, as the conversation was nearing an end, she added, "One more thing, preacher. When they bury me, I want my old Bible in one hand and a fork in the other."

"A fork?" This caught the pastor by surprise. "Why do you want to be buried with a fork?"

She explained that at some of the most memorable church dinners and banquets she had attended over her lifetime, someone would tell the guests, "You can keep your fork." That meant that dessert was coming—the good stuff, like chocolate cake or cherry pie. So when people saw her in her casket and wondered, *What's with the fork?,* she wanted him to tell them to keep their forks, because the best was yet to come![56]

The Apostle Paul wrote, "I always pray with joy . . . being confident of this, that he who began a good work in you will carry it on to completion until the day of Christ Jesus." That was *his* way of saying, "The best is yet to come." And a bit later in the same letter, Paul added, "I do not consider myself yet to have taken hold of [my goal]. But one thing I do: Forgetting what is behind and straining toward what is ahead, I press on toward the goal to win the prize for which God has called me heavenward in Christ Jesus" (Philippians 3:13-14).

We must press toward our goals, run to win, strain to get there. Yet while doing so, we can be at peace knowing that He will complete what He started in us. My prayer and earnest desire for you is that you won't just go through the motions and let the fear of "what if" scare you into settling for what is. I believe God can, will, and desires to do exceedingly abundantly more in and through your life, if you let Him. And the beautiful thing is that all He asks is your submission and surrender.

POSSIBILITIES ARE ENDLESS

I remember sitting across from a young man years ago and asked him who he had in his corner to encourage him for the road ahead. He looked dead into my eyes and said, "The only person I have in my corner is you."

I was stunned, but his stark statement also motivated me. I do want people to know I'm in their corner because as we've affirmed throughout this book, life can be very hard. It can be challenging. It can be very painful and at times unfair. However, my prayer is that you'll always remember that God has blessed you with more power and potential buried deep inside your soul than you can even imagine. God has given you unique experiences and passions. He has entrusted you with a specific and strategic plan, and has set before you a purpose that only you can fulfill. Your family, your friends, and this world need what perhaps only you can offer.

Martin Luther King, Jr. once said, "The ultimate measure of a man is not where he stands in moments of comfort and convenience, but where he stands at times of challenge and controversy." Some of you right now are in that season of friction and discomfort—that season of challenge and difficulty. But I want to suggest that maybe it's time to stop asking, "God, why do You have me here?" and ask instead, "God, what do You want me to learn while You have me here?" Sometimes life's greatest treasures are hidden among life's most painful circumstances. I believe God has something for you to learn exactly where you are now, and the beautiful thing is that no matter how far you stray, wander, or sink, you're never out of His reach.

Several years ago as my wife and I were watching *America's Got Talent*, we fell in love (along with the rest of the nation) with one of the contestants named Jane Marczewski, better known as "Nightbirde." We were heartbroken, yet inspired, by Jane's story of having gone through some very tumultuous times . . . a broken marriage, dreams deferred, and then on top of that, her battle with cancer. Yet even during all those hardships, Jane exuded an overwhelming and unspeakable joy.

I believe Jane put an "even if. . ." faith on full display. She knew where her identity was ultimately rooted and found. She knew that although life was incredibly hard and challenging, she could find rest in the One who had already proclaimed victory. Jane wrote one of the most profound blog posts I've ever read, called *God Is on the Bathroom Floor*. It wasn't written out of a place of ease or during a mountaintop moment with God. Rather, she wrote like the psalmists who were feeling excruciating pain, yet chose to see their circumstances from a different perspective.[57]

It doesn't matter if you're on the mountaintop or in the deepest, darkest valley you've ever endured, God is with you. He isn't just some distant authoritarian figure up in heaven who leaves us to handle all our challenges. No, He goes before us, keeps watch behind us, and walks beside us every step of the way. He's aware of every sleepless night, every tear-filled heartache, and every discouraging and disappointing moment you face.

Pastor Mark Batterson once shared on our *Built Different* podcast that the way you can assess someone's spiritual maturity is by whether they can see "the miraculous in the midst of the monotonous." Just because you can't see it doesn't mean God is not at work preparing and developing your miracle.

One final lesson for those who desire to develop an "even if. . ." mindset comes from one of my former collegiate strength coaches, Shelton Stevens, who has over seventeen years of coaching experience and currently serves as a Human Performance Specialist for the United States Army Special Operations Command. He taught me that motivation and discipline are two very different things. Motivation is fleeting, feelings-based, and external. Someone can be very motivated one day and not at all the next. But discipline is the pursuit of inner excellence every single day of your life—a standard that you hold yourself to. Living a disciplined life is essential for those who are in pursuit of something greater because discipline will take you places motivation never could.

Still, there's no question that we live in a feelings-based society. We do difficult things only when we feel like it. Consider the statistics that have been accumulated about new year's resolutions. Researchers have found that only nine percent of Americans that make new year's resolutions ever complete them. Almost a fourth of them (23 percent) quit by the end of the first week, and that total is up to 43 percent by the end of January.[58]

Anyone can make a commitment, but not everyone can remain consistent. I love what Denzel Washington once said, "Without commitment, you'll never start. But more importantly, without consistency, you'll never finish."[59]

To help build a greater level of consistency in my own life, over the last several years I have taken the Jon Gordon approach of choosing to reflect on and live by one word throughout the calendar year. As I prayed and prayed about what God wanted me to reflect on last year, the word *discipline* came to my mind. I wanted to become more disciplined in my physical, mental, relational, and spiritual health and wellbeing. After spending the year pondering that word, here's the most important thing I learned about discipline: *Desire is not a requirement of doing.* I can assure you that you'll face days when you lack the desire, but that shouldn't stop you from doing the right thing. As the author of Hebrews wrote, "No discipline seems pleasant at the time, but painful. Later on, however, it produces a harvest of righteousness and peace for those who have been trained by it" (Hebrews 12:11).

As you come to the end of this book, my prayer is that you don't just feel encouraged and motivated, but rather that you have been informed and equipped to cultivate and develop an "even if . . ." perspective that will reshape the trajectory of your life. You will start to view obstacles as opportunities. You will continue to prepare for future opportunities. You will be able to praise God during your painful times, even before your breakthrough. You will be more selective about those you allow to impact and influence your life. When you truly believe that God is at your side, the possibilities are endless.

Know this: God has an incredible plan and purpose for your life. He is not finished with you yet. I challenge you to live a life that will be worth remembering, a contagious life that makes people ask, "What does that person have that I don't?" And by all means, share the love and grace of God that you receive with others who need it.

A dear friend and mentor of mine, Jay Strack, once challenged me: "Don't commit the sin of the desert." He had to explain to me that the sin of the desert is when you know where the water is, but you don't share that information. If God has revealed more of himself to you through the pages of this book, tell others about the everlasting water He provides.

Finally, I want to leave you with an example to follow. Habakkuk remains unknown to many people because he is tucked away amid all the other minor prophets at the end of the Old Testament, yet he exemplifies essentially everything I've been writing about. Not unlike Job, he approached God with some very difficult questions concerning the unfairness of life, listened to God's responses, and came away with a new perspective. By the end of his short book, he writes:

> **Though the fig tree does not bud and there are no grapes on the vines,**

> though the olive crop fails and the fields produce no food,
> though there are no sheep in the pen and no cattle in the
>   stalls,
> yet I will rejoice in the Lord, I will be joyful in God my Savior.
> (Habakkuk 3:17-18)

I think it's fair to substitute "even if" for "though" in all three instances. The lesson is the same. Habakkuk had some very serious concerns and no immediate answers, yet he was convinced of God's presence and God's power. His "even if . . ." mindset allowed him to see beyond the current disasters and not only acknowledge, but *rejoice* in his God. My prayer is that we all will learn to do the same.

Jesus Christ is the same yesterday and today and forever (Hebrews 13:8). He didn't come to free you from the fight; He came to free you *for* the fight! Keep seeking your peace and power in His presence, setting your eyes on things above to fuel your newfound perspective. And above all, never give up, because wherever God has you, He can mightily use you!

Keep believing.

Keep praying.

Keep praising.

And keep your fork, because your best is yet to come.

ENDNOTES

1   https://www.youtube.com/watch?v=8PzQmtwNeXM

2   Find more comprehensive details in Marcus Luttrell's autobiography, *Lone Survivor: The Eyewitness Account of Operation Red Wings and the Lost Heroes of SEAL Team 10* (New York: Little, Brown and Company, 2007), the 2013 film *Lone Survivor*, and at https://www.usamm.com/blogs/news/the-navys-official-account-of-operation-red-wings

3   Jon Gordon and Damon West, *How to Be a Coffee Bean: 111 Life-Changing Ways to Create Positive Change* (Hoboken, NJ: Wiley, 2023), p. xiv

4   Rory Vaden, "Be the Buffalo and Face Life's Storms," *The Tennessean*, Jan. 23, 2015, www.tennessean.com/story/money/2015/01/23/buffalo-face-lifes-storms/22187351/

5   Lance Armstrong, quoted in Eric Thomas, *You Owe You* (New York: Rodale, 2022), p. 143

6   C.S. Lewis, *The Problem of Pain* (New York, Macmillan, 1962), p. 93

7   Homer, *The Odyssey*, Book 9

8   Charles E. Hummel, *Tyranny of the Urgent* (Downers Grove, IL: InterVarsity Press, 1967), p. 5

9   C.S. Lewis, *The Weight of Glory* (New York: HarperOne, 1949), p. 27

10 Dane C. Ortlund, *Deeper: Real Change for Real Sinners* (Wheaton, IL: Crossway, 2021), p. 139

11 Michael Parrish, "10-Year-Old with Matches Started a California Wildfire," *New York Times*, Nov. 1, 2004 https://www.nytimes.com/2007/11/01/us/01wildfire.html

12 C.S. Lewis, *Mere Christianity* (New York: HarperCollins, 1952), p. 100

13 Debbie Moore, "Sin Fascinates, Assassinates, Adrian Rogers Tells Seminarians," *Baptist Press*, Aug. 31, 2000, https://www.baptistpress. com/resource-library/news/sin-fascinates-assassinates-adrian-rogers-tells-seminarians/#:~:text=If%20ministers%20do%20not%20 stay,Sin%20is%20so%20deceitful.%E2%80%9D

14 Charles Haddon Spurgeon, "*Morning and Evening: Daily Readings*," 1928, p. 536

15 Matthew Henry, *Concise Commentary on the Whole Bible* (Nashville: Thomas Nelson, 2003), entry for Judges 16:22

16 Steve Brown, *Three Free Sins: God's Not Mad at You* (New York: Howard Books, 2012), pp. 37-39

17 Brennan Manning, *Ruthless Trust: The Ragamuffin's Path to God* (New York: HarperSanFrancisco, 2000), p. 12

18 Edwin Louis Cole, *Maximized Manhood: A Guide to Family Survival* (New Kensington, PA: Whitaker House, 1982), p. 72

19 Mel Johnson, "Bystanders Too Afraid to Save Man Trapped in Fiery Crash & Then Angel Shows Up Just in Time," GodUpdates, July 31, 2019, https://www.godupdates.com/fiery-crash-rescue-tim-vachon/

20 John C. Maxwell, "John C. Maxwell on Finding Your Purpose," *Success*, June 27, 2022, https://www.success.com/finding-your-purpose/

21 "'I fight for milk'—Jim Braddock," *The Business Beacon*, September 15, 2010, https://abacusandco.wordpress. com/2010/09/15/%E2%80%9Ci-fight-for-milk%E2%80%9D-%E2%80%93-jim-braddock/

22 Johnson, I., & Hagood, J., *Inky: An amazing story of faith and perseverance* (29:11 Publications, 2011)

23 Inky Johnson, cited in "How You View What You Do," *Self-Improvement Daily*, Sept. 16, 2022, https://www.selfimprovementdailytips.com/podcast/how-you-view-what-you-do

24 Tim S. Grover, *Relentless: From Good to Great to Unstoppable* (New York: Scribner, 2013), p. 119

25 Charles H. Spurgeon, "Faith and Its Attendant Privilege," Answers in Genesis https://answersingenesis.org/education/spurgeon-sermons/1203-faith-and-its-attendant-privilege/

26 Richard Foster, *Celebration of Discipline: The Path to Spiritual Growth* (New York: HarperCollins, 1978) pp. 5-7

27 Richard Feloni, "Tim Ferriss Lives His Life According to an Ancient Greek Quote That Helps Him Prepare for the Worst," *Business Insider*, Dec. 1, 2017, https://www.businessinsider.com/tim-ferriss-favorite-quote-greek-philosopher-archilochus-2017-12

28 Michael Jordan, cited in RingCentral blog, Jan. 30, 2023, https://www.ringcentral.com/us/en/blog/some-people-want-it-to-happen-some-wish-it-would-happen-others-make-it-happen-michael-jordan/

29 Richard Needham, *The Wit and Wisdom of Richard Needham* (Edmonton, Alberta: Hurtig, 1977) cited in Thuita J. Maina, "Mistakes That Made Me Grow," *Reflections of a Young Man*, Mar. 6, 2019, https://thuitamaina.com/selected_story.php?Index=118

30 From a post on Twitter (X), Jan. 5, 2023, Accessed Jan 6, 2024 https://twitter.com/TimTebow/status/1611113100941611008?lang=en

31 A.B. Simpson, *Days of Heaven upon Earth: A Year Book of Scripture Texts and Living Truths* (New York: Christian Alliance Publishing Company, 1897), p. 214 cited in "Inspirational Thought of the Day," For the Love of God Oasis Bible Ministry, July 27, 2022, https://forgodslove52.com/2022/07/27/ephesians-412-a-b-simpson/

32 "Walk-off: Alabama Beats Georgia in OT for National Title," ESPN, Jan. 9, 2018, https://www.espn.com/college-football/recap/_/gameId/400953415

33   Jon Gordon, *The Power of Positive Leadership* (Hoboken, NJ; Wiley, 2017), https://www.appleseeds.org/Gordon_Show-Up-Do-the-Work.htm

34   John Maxwell, *The Maxwell Leadership Bible* (Nashville: Thomas Nelson, 2014), p. 67

35   "Jalen Hurts plays hero as Alabama stuns Georgia with late rally in SEC championship," Dan Wolken, *USA Today*, December 1, 2018

36   "Jalen Hurts recalls being benched for Tua Tagovailoa at Alabama," Brad Crawford, 247sports.com, March 8, 2020

37   Smith, E., "Lunchbreak: Kirk Cousins ranked among NFL's most accurate QBs," 2020. https://www.vikings.com/news/kirk-cousins-ranked-among-nfl-most-accurate-qbs

38   My interview with Kirk took place at the March 2018 Ignite Men's Impact Weekend. Find out more about Kirk on his website (kirk-cousins.org), where the first thing you'll see is Proverbs 3:5-6.

39   John Wesley, *John Wesley's Explanatory Notes on the Whole Bible*, "Commentary on Genesis 39," Entry for Genesis 39:20, StudyLight. org, https://www.studylight.org/commentaries/eng/wen/genesis-39.html#verse-20

40   James Prochaska, John Norcross, and Carlo DiClemente, "Changing for Good: A Revolutionary Six-Step Program for Overcoming Bad Habits and Moving Your Life Positively Forward," *F5 Financial Planning*, https://www.f5fp.com/wp-content/uploads/2014/12/Changing-for-Good-Prochaska-Norcross-DiClemente.pdf

41   David Goggins, "Powerful Motivational Speech Video with David Goggins," *Eightify*, https://eightify.app/summary/motivation-and-inspiration/powerful-motivational-speech-video-with-david-goggins#:~:text=The%20best%20feeling%20of%20victory,of%20external%20factors%20or%20resources.&text=-%22We%20all%20look%20for%20toughness,toughness%20in%20a%20comfortable%20environment.%22

42   Amy Culver, "The Inspiring Life Story of KFC's Colonel Sanders," snagajob, Aug. 1, 2023, https://www.snagajob.com/blog/post/the-inspiring-life-story-of-kfcs-colonel-sanders

43   "Colonel Harland Sanders: Founder of Kentucky Fried Chicken," University of Houston Conrad N. Hilton College of Global Hospitality Leadership, Accessed Jan. 3, 2024, https://uh.edu/hilton-college/About/Hospitality-Industry-Hall-of-Honor/Inductees/Colonel-Harland-Sanders%20/

44   Craig Groeschel, *The Power to Change* (Grand Rapids, MI: Zondervan, 2023), p. 30

45   Aikansh Chaudhary, "Michael Jordon's Smart Response to What Makes Him Special," *Fadeaway World*, Nov. 24, 2022, https://fadeawayworld.net/nba-media/michael-jordans-smart-response-to-what-makes-him-special

46   Mark Stewart, *Hard to the Hoop* (Kildare, Ireland: Millbrook Press, 2000), p. 46

47   Max Davis, *The Insanity of Unbelief: A Journalist's Journey from Belief, to Skepticism, to Deep Faith* (Shippensburg, PA: Destiny Image, 2013)

48   The Voice of the Martyrs, *I Am N: Inspiring Stories of Christians Facing Islamic Extremists* (Colorado Springs: David C. Cook, 2016), pp. 105-108

49   "Daniel 6," *Lange Commentary on the Holy Scriptures*, Entry for Daniel 6:25 [24], https://biblehub.com/commentaries/lange/daniel/6.htm

50   C.S. Lewis, *The Weight of Glory* (New York: HarperOne, 1949), pp. 182-183

51   Charles Stanley, cited in George Sweeting, *Who Said That?* (Chicago: Moody Press, 1994), p. 364

52   Rick Warren, *The Purpose Driven Life* (Grand Rapids: Zondervan, 2002), p. 265

53   Charles Spurgeon, "Satanic Hindrances," *Metropolitan Tabernacle Pulpit Volume 11*, The Spurgeon Center, October 29, 1865, https://www.spurgeon.org/resource-library/sermons/satanic-hindrances/#flipbook/

54   Sidney Poitier, *The Measure of a Man: A Spiritual Autobiography* (New York: HarperSanFrancisco, 2000), p. 19

55   Jon Gordon and Damon West, *How to Be a Coffee Bean: 111 Life-Changing Ways to Create Positive Change* (Hoboken, NJ: Wiley, 2023), p. xiv

56   Roger William Thomas, "Keep Your Fork," cited in Jack Canfield and Mark Victor Hansen (Eds.), *A 3rd Serving of Chicken Soup for the Soul*, pp. 186-188

57   Nightbirde's "God Is on the Bathroom Floor" can be found at www.nightbirde.co/blog/2021/9/27/god-is-on-the-bathroom-floor

58   Emma Pitts, "How to Make Your 2024 New Year's Resolutions Stick, *Deseret News*, Nov. 30, 2023, https://www.deseret.com/2023/11/30/23983201/how-to-make-resolution-stick-habits-new-years

59   Denzel Washington, 2017 NAACP Image Awards, Speakola, Feb. 11, 2017, https://speakola.com/arts/denzel-washington-naacp-image-awards-2017

ACKNOWLEDGEMENTS

God has strategically placed a number of "even if" people in my life. I'm grateful to each one who has helped strengthen, shape, and encourage me along the way.

To my best friend and wife, Evelyn Jane. You have been a beacon of light and hope in my life since the day we met. I love you so much. I pray that the principles of this book will be the heartbeat of our marriage and family for all of our days.

To Dad and Mom. I can't even begin to express my love and appreciation for both of you. Thank you for consistently displaying an "even if" faith, mindset, and endurance every day of my life. This book wouldn't have been possible without the example you continually set and the love and devotion you've invested in me. No words will ever express the depth of my gratitude.

To Ben, Megan, Olivia, and Sophia. I'm grateful that I don't just get to call you family but also best friends. Evelyn and I love you dearly, and I so appreciate the love and support you've shown me throughout my life. I pray for you every day, and I will always be in your corner.

To Max Davis. What a joy it has been working alongside you to make this book come to life. You are a blessing to the church, and this book would have just been a dream if it weren't for you and your efforts. I cannot thank you enough for the way you embrace your calling in using your gifts and talents to share the testimonies of others as you continually spread the Good News of the gospel.

To Pat Springle, Stan Campbell, Jennifer Ellers, Garrett Hedrick, Trenton Haddock, and our entire AACC Publishing Team. Thank you for your dedication, hard work, and efforts to make this book a reality. I'm grateful for the way each of you contributed throughout this process.

To the rest of my Clinton and Sherman family, friends, coaches, mentors, podcast interviewees, and more. Thank you for the positive imprint you've left on my life. Again, this message would not have been possible without the lessons I've learned from you. Thank you for who you are, what you do, and how you've loved me throughout this journey.

Lastly, and most importantly, I want to thank my Lord and Savior, Jesus Christ. Thank You for loving me and choosing me . . . in spite of me. The decision to follow You and live my life for You will always be the greatest decision I'll ever make. Thank You for the mountain tops, but I especially, thank You for the valleys, because it's been those challenging, dark, and lonely times when You have revealed just how loving and caring You truly are. Those moments have taught me the lessons about what it means to live by the mantra: "even if."

ABOUT THE AUTHOR

Zach Clinton is a rising voice in this generation, one who believes in every person's capacity to meet challenges, rise above adversity, and help people chase after their dreams. His thirst for excellence started as a young athlete and aspiring competitor. He was a dynamic three-sport athlete who quickly became a student of the games, taking him to Division 1 collegiate athletics. That hunger, passion, and calling still shine bright in his heart as he has become a student of performance and motivational psychology—helping people understand themselves and achieve greatness.

Serving as the Vice President of the American Association of Christian Counselors, President and Host of Ignite Men's Impact Weekend, Host of the renowned "Built Different Podcast," and Licensed Resident Counselor in the state of Virginia, Zach has a heart for the broken and hurting, as well as those who aspire to unlock their highest potential. More than anything, Zach wants to remind people they're never alone and never out of the fight!

Zach is a proud husband of his best friend and wife, Evelyn. They have a real love for serving others and spreading the Good News of the gospel. Zach's prayer is that through this book you would be filled with hope, encouragement, and the drive to shed the "what if" and "only if" limitations and choose an "even if" faith and endurance for the journey ahead.

RESOURCES

To order more copies of this book,
go to Amazon.com or www.aacc.net

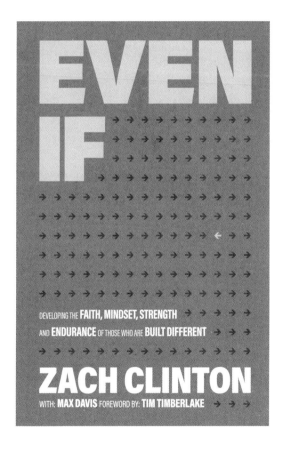

"She speaks wisely, teaching with gracious love."
— Proverbs 31:26 (ISV)

extraordinary
women

Extraordinary Women exists to help draw women closer to the heart of God...every day. Extraordinary Women is not just a Christian women's event...it's a lifestyle. We are excited that women attend our conferences, but we want more than just a few days with you. We want to be a part of your life! Follow us on your favorite social media platforms and sign up to receive a free 10 day devotional series.

Our desire is to encourage your heart and help you draw closer to the heart of God every day.

Julie Clinton
President, Extraordinary Women

www.ewomen.net · 800.526.8673

 Facebook.com/ewomen   Twitter.com/ewomen   Instagram.com/ewomen.ministries

Become a Mental Health Coach! Over 15,000 churches and 30,000 students enrolled!

CERTIFIED
Mental Health Coach
FIRST RESPONDER TRAINING

LIMITED TIME SCHOLARSHIP
No cost to the church and tuition is FREE for students!
(One-time $54 tech support fee applies)

"Without question, this training will be one of the most, if not the most, significant projects we have ever done in the history of the AACC. We need an army of helpers in the local church—those of whom God has given natural gifts and talents to offer help, hope, and guidance to the hurting!"

Dr. Tim Clinton, President
American Association of Christian Counselors

Introducing the Mental Health Coach Training, a 42-hour, biblically-based training that consists of three courses. Enroll and successfully complete all three courses and become a **"Certified Mental Health Coach"** by the International Board of Christian Care.

Our 2023 mission is to engage, educate and equip an additional 6,500 churches and congregations and to train 45,000 students all over America and around the world.

Who can enroll? Under the discretion of your church, **anyone with a calling to offer help, hope, and encouragement** to those who are hurting and looking for guidance and direction in everyday life.

- 42-hour, Biblically-based, clinically-excellent training program
- Featuring some of the world's leading mental health and ministry experts
- Study anywhere, anytime, at your own pace, on any of your favorite devices!
- On-demand video lectures—No schedules!
- Available 24/7/365
- And you have one year to complete your course

Learn to help those who struggle with **Serious Mental Illness (SMI),** including topics like:

- Addiction
- Trauma and Abuse
- Grief and Loss
- Boundaries
- Panic Disorders
- PTSD
- Phobias
- Suicide
- Crisis Intervention
- Depression
- Stress and Anxiety
  ... and more!

LIGHTUNIVERSITY.COM/MENTALHEALTHCOACH

6-Week Introductory Study of Biblical Counseling

COFFEE CUP COUNSELING
training program

Anger, Depression, Stress, Loss, Betrayal...

A Six-Week Introductory Study of Biblical Counseling
(complete with a leader's guide)

Coffee Cup COFFEE CUP
Counseling
Learning to Care for People God's Way

TIM CLINTON & PAT SPRINGLE

COFFEE CUP
Counseling

DVD

"WHAT TO SAY WHEN YOU DON'T
KNOW WHAT TO SAY;
WHAT TO DO WHEN YOU DON'T
KNOW WHAT TO DO."

Lessons Include:

Week 1: Caring for People in Need
Tim Clinton, Ed.D.

Week 2: Models of Care
Ron Hawkins, D.Min., Ed.D.

Week 3: Becoming a Great Listener
Mercy Connors, Ph.D.

Week 4: Relying on the Scriptures and Prayer
Ron Hawkins, D.Min., Ed.D.

Week 5: Resources and Referrals
Mercy Connors, Ph.D.

Week 6: Getting Started
Tim Clinton, Ed.D.

In the six weeks of training, you'll learn:

- The privilege and responsibility of stepping into people's lives when they're most vulnerable
- The biblical basis of caring friendships
- A time-tested, three-step model of helping
- How to care for people in times of crisis
- How to become a skilled and effective listener
- How to address the difficult issues of abuse and boundaries
- How to establish a network of competent professionals for referrals
- And many other insights and practical skills you can use!

1-800-526-8673 • AACC.NET

HOPE & HEALING SERIES

The authors of these workbooks write with clinical insights and personal warmth, and they provide practical applications. Each workbook is designed for individual reflection, counseling interactions, and group discussions.

They are available on Amazon or at aacc.net

THE CHRISTIAN COUNSELING WORKBOOK SERIES
A Guide to Help Overcome Life's Challenging Moments

HOPE & HEALING FOR DEPRESSION

GREGORY L. JANTZ, PH.D
WITH KEITH WALL

THE CHRISTIAN COUNSELING WORKBOOK SERIES
A Guide to Healing Through Loss

HOPE & HEALING FOR GRIEF

WRITTEN BY
KEVIN ELLERS, D. MIN.

THE CHRISTIAN COUNSELING WORKBOOK SERIES
A Guide to Holistic Recovery

HOPE & HEALING FOR FOOD ADDICTION

WRITTEN BY
RHONA EPSTEIN, PSY.D

THE CHRISTIAN COUNSELING WORKBOOK SERIES
A Guide to Help Flourish in Community

HOPE & HEALING FOR LONELINESS

WRITTEN BY
MARK MAYFIELD, PH.D